Computerization
and the Transformation
of Employment

Computerization and the Transformation of Employment

Government, Hospitals, and Universities

Thomas M. Stanback, Jr.

Westview Press / Boulder and London

Conservation of Human Resources Studies in the New Economy

Published in 1987 in the United States of America by Westview Press, Inc.; Frederick A. Praeger, Publisher; 5500 Central Avenue, Boulder, Colorado 80301

Library of Congress Cataloging-in-Publication Data
Stanback, Thomas M., Jr.
  Computerization and the transformation of employment.
  (Conservation of human resources studies in the
new economy)
  Includes bibliographies and index.
  1. Corporations, Nonprofit—United States—Management
—Data processing. I. Title. II. Series.
HD62.6.S73 1987   658'.048'0285   86-22372
ISBN 0-8133-7320-4 (alk. paper)

Composition for this book was created by conversion of the author's computer tapes or word-processor disks.

Printed and bound in the United States of America

 The paper used in this publication meets the requirements of the American National Standard for Permanence of Paper for Printed Library Materials Z39.48-1984.

6   5   4   3   2   1

To Margaret

Contents

Tables and Figures

Tables

Figures

ix

Foreword

Two decades have passed since the Conservation of Human Resources, Columbia University, published *The Pluralistic Economy* (Eli Ginzberg, Dale L. Hiestand, and Beatrice G. Reubens, 1965). Important ties link this earlier investigation to the present book by Thomas M. Stanback, Jr., which reports on the current status and future prospects for computerization in the not-for-profit sector, that is, the governmental and nonprofit arenas combined.

The authors of *The Pluralistic Economy* called attention, for the first time, to the flaws in the conventional model of the U.S. economy. According to the conventional view, the economy consisted of a predominant private sector and a small government sector. The model failed to allow for a significant third sector—the nonprofit sector—which plays a leading role in such critical fields as health care (hospitalization), higher education, and cultural activities (museums, orchestras, opera, etc.), as well as religious institutions and a broad array of social welfare organizations.

Furthermore, analysis of national product and employment data revealed that the not-for-profit sector accounted for between one-quarter and one-third of gross national product and between one-third and two-fifths of employment. These proportions challenged the established view that the private sector dominated and provided the motivating power of the U.S. economy.

It is no accident that this conventional belief dominated public opinion for such a long period even after investigations had challenged it. Economists who developed and propagated the private-sector model—with help from business, politicians, and the press—have long been wedded to the conviction that the U.S. economy has been and remains a basically competitive economy dominated by competitive markets. The existence of multinational corporations such as GE, Exxon, IBM, GM, and many others supports this model.

Ideology played the key role in the continuing dominance of the private-sector model. But it was the lack of sensitivity among opinion leaders to the critical importance of such infrastructure institutions as government, health care organizations, and colleges and universities that reinforced the model. To this very day, the U.S. economic system is known as "capitalism," which suggests that financial and physical capital are the key inputs into the system. But the facts are otherwise. More than 80 percent of national income is paid out each year in the form of wages and salaries, benefits, and the labor earnings of the self-employed. Returns to property, including interest, amount to less than 20 percent.

Another serious shortcoming of the conventional model is that it neglects the role of services, which today account for roughly 70 percent of the nation's output and jobs. Along with Marxists, market economists have often placed a faulty emphasis on commodity production. They have denigrated and disregarded the role of services both as final products and as transforming agents in a specialized economy.

In this important book, Stanback explores the role of computerization in the not-for-profit sector—a sector that accounts for a significant proportion of the nation's income and employment and provides a range of essential services. The not-for-profit sector not only ensures the continued dynamism of the economy, but also satisfies the critical needs and desires of the public.

To reiterate the above points from a somewhat different vantage: Without properly functioning municipal governments, the contemporary U.S. economy (in which roughly 70 percent of the population lives in Standard Metropolitan Statistical Areas) could not exist, much less flourish. It is difficult to conceive of what life would be like in the United States if steadily improving health and educational services were not available.

So much for setting the scene. Let us now look more closely at the theme that Stanback sets forth in this book. He focuses on the impact of computerization on the restructuring of work in municipal government, hospitals, and universities and colleges. Specifically, he assesses not only the impact of technology on patterns of work, but also on the impact of the changed production cycle on workers and their careers.

His findings, greatly oversimplified and generalized, are:

1. New technology is opening up important frontiers in each of three important industries. These breakthroughs result in new outputs, lower costs, improved quality, and new work assignments that for the most part lead to skill-expansion rather than skill-contraction.

There is nothing simple, quick, or inexpensive about implementing the new technology and tuning it to where it is fully functional. Installing a computer system usually takes sizable investments in capital; retraining existing staffs takes time; and getting the management and the work force to accept technology as a friend and not as a threat takes even more time.

2. From a theoretical standpoint, Stanback questions William Baumol's thesis that the service sector is characterized by "cost disease," by which Baumol meant that since services depend so greatly on labor inputs, they cannot benefit from the rationalization that characterizes the commodity sector, where machinery can be used to cut costs. Service outputs eventually will be constrained by their ever-rising absolute and relative costs. But Stanback argues that Baumol's view of services is flawed and that the economics profession, which, for the most part, had accepted Baumol's view, has been misled in assessing services. Stanback presents overwhelming evidence that these critical services can be rationalized, costs reduced, and the value of output per unit of input enhanced.

3. Another important result of Stanback's work is his recognition of the time factor involved in introducing new technology. The capacity of the computer to change the way work is performed in the three industries does not mean that those in a position to set policy will jump at the opportunity to introduce technology. Many employees in senior positions are reluctant to change their ways. Stanback notes that considerable time must pass before managers in top positions have had the training and experience to embrace a new technology wholeheartedly. How quickly they accept new technology will, of course, be influenced by the competitive pressures they confront. Stanback argues persuasively that in the face of resistance to higher taxes by U.S. citizens, third-party payer pressures on hospitals for cost containment, and the financial vulnerability of institutions of higher learning in a period of declining enrollments, many senior managers are likely to be persuaded to move quickly to adopt the new technology but may nevertheless delay because of the costs of capital.

4. Stanback notes that management in the not-for-profit sector usually faces greater difficulties in acquiring the capital needed for investment than is true in the for-profit sector. In the for-profit sector, the investment funds are usually readily obtainable if management can demonstrate that the new technology will pay for itself within a stipulated period of time.

5. One of Stanback's more interesting findings relates to the issue of worker displacement. He has found little or no evidence to support the widespread belief that the computer will displace a large number of workers. Moreover, he has found little evidence to support the related fear that the computer results in downskilling or turns responsible jobs into routine operations.

6. But I must quickly add that not all of Stanback's findings are saccharine. He points out that the restructuring of work, particularly in

government and hospitals, is likely to lead in time to the elimination of many simple, routine clerical jobs. That being the case, he questions what will happen to the large number of poorly educated persons who previously found a toehold in the economy by being hired for such jobs. In the case of the government of New York City, many employees who started at the bottom have enjoyed, in years past, opportunities to move up not one but several rungs. Stanback's answer goes as follows: The basic schooling available to the urban poor must be improved; employers undergoing computerization must provide ample opportunities for the retraining of personnel whose old jobs are being restructured; employers must be careful not to establish unrealistic requirements for entry-level jobs; and the community college structure needs to be broadened and access kept open so that those on the bottom rungs can acquire additional competences that will help them advance.

There is much more in Stanback's book, which represents an excellent admixture of broad theoretical understanding and rich case materials. Moreover, his prose is straightforward, and the reader will have no problem in following his argument. I take much pleasure and, based on our research relationship of more than two decades, much pride in commending this interesting and important book to a wide readership.

Eli Ginzberg, Director
Conservation of Human Resources,
Columbia University

Acknowledgments

Any study that relies heavily on interview material is likely to leave the author in the debt of many who gave freely of their time. This book is no exception, and I regret that it is not feasible to name each person who contributed information, encouragement, or criticism along the way. There are several, however, who made major contributions and must be acknowledged. Richard Davidoff, head of New York City's Office of Computer Plans and Controls, gave freely of his time in providing extensive background on the city's computerization efforts. The late Joseph Kroculick of Columbia University's Center for Computing Activities reviewed the university's experience in light of the development of computer technology. Both read and criticized the manuscript.

At the Conservation of Human Resources Project, Miriam Ostow and Howard Berliner provided background on the special problems of hospitals and critically reviewed the manuscript. But, as always during the past two decades of association with the Conservation of Human Resources staff, my greatest debt is to Eli Ginzberg for his encouragement, incisive criticism, and warm personal support.

I am also grateful to Shoshana Vasheetz and Ellen Levine for their patience and skill in typing the manuscript and to Penny Peace for a thorough editing of the work, which significantly improved its style.

Financial support for the study was provided by the Ford Foundation.

Thomas M. Stanback, Jr.

1

Computerization and Work: An Overview

As we enter the late 1980s, it is clear that the U.S. economy is caught up in a technological revolution centered on the computer and tele-communications that is altering radically the ways in which we produce goods and services, the organization of businesses and institutions, and the content of work. Among these various dimensions of change the impacts on employment are perhaps the most important and the most in need of study. High general levels of unemployment, even under conditions of cyclical prosperity, and much higher levels of seemingly intractable minority unemployment, coupled with major shifts toward white-collar and part-time work, raise new questions regarding the kinds of career opportunities a new generation of workers is facing and will continue to face in the years ahead.

In this book I examine evidence relating to the impact of the new technology on nonprofit organizations, a major sector of the U.S. economy characterized by rising costs and generally regarded as labor intensive and relatively unproductive. Three groups of organizations are studied: municipal government (as represented by New York City), hospitals, and colleges and universities.

The objectives of the study are twofold: (1) to shed light on the impact of computerization on employment in terms of changes in the nature of work and career opportunities (i.e., what a person does in a given job, what training, experience, or native aptitude is required and what opportunities exist for upward mobility) and changes in the distribution of occupations (i.e., which occupations are becoming rel-atively more, or relatively less, important); and (2) to assess the pace at which changes in employment are occurring as a result of technological applications and related organizational change.

The empirical portion of this book is based largely on interviews, principally with administrators and professionals at various levels of user organizations, but also, for background, with knowledgeable persons such as equipment vendors, employment agency executives, and consultants. These interviews not only yield bits and scraps of hard employment data but also provide a rich source of information on the extent to which computerization has progressed, how procedures are being changed, how workers adapt to new requirements through training or reassignment, the changes occurring in managerial attitudes, and the overall effectiveness of computer applications in getting the job done. In addition, the interviews provide information concerning the applications underway. New systems are not put into place overnight. Budgets must be approved, software written, hardware procured, strategies mapped, and workers trained or recruited. A knowledge of projects underway helps to foretell what lies ahead for some time to come.

The Nature of Technological Revolution: An Approach to Analysis

Alvin Toffler has argued that Western societies are in the initial stage of a "third wave" of change—the information revolution—centered around computer technology. (The first wave was the agrarian revolution and the second the industrial).[1] Whether or not one agrees with this interpretation of history, there is impressive evidence that the magnitude of the changes being wrought by the computer, combined with new telecommunication and video technologies, is comparable to earlier major eras of technological change (e.g., steam, electrical, automotive). The changes are being diffused throughout virtually every productive activity. If this is indeed the case, certain generalizations can be drawn from past experience that give perspective to the current experience and provide a framework for analysis.

The first generalization is that a technological revolution is cumulative and self-reinforcing. This principle is true because the revolution is driven by both technological and human factors. Technologically, the revolution is based not on a single invention but on a series of advances, each made possible by the success of its forerunners and inherent in the technology itself. Each advance offers higher levels of effectiveness and cost efficiency as well as a broader range of applications. On the human side, the revolution is driven by enthusiasm and changing expectations. As managers and workers learn new skills and begin to understand the new technology, they tend to want to use it and broaden its applications. Generations of managers emerge determined to stake their futures on new methods of production, and ventures centered on the new technology proliferate. At the same time, the younger workers readily accept the emergent technology and give preference to employment in the more productive modern firms and institutions.

The second generalization to be drawn from past experience is that the revolution is constrained by costs, infrastructural inadequacies, and, once again, human considerations. New technology involves extensive capital expenditures. But the funding is not always readily available even when expected returns are attractive. Application may also require the time-consuming and expensive construction of capital infrastructures (e.g., rails, highways, electrical generating equipment, and transmission lines in older technologies). Finally, on the human side, adoption of technology may be hobbled by managers who lack understanding of the potentials, by risk aversion and incapacity to effect the necessary institutional reorganization, and by the daunting problems of retraining workers and interrupting existing procedures and workflows.

The third and final generalization is that technological revolutions tend to involve considerable adaptation and compromise. The conflict between the imperative to adopt the new and the hesitancy to act are mediated by arrangements that prolong the process of change by adapting the new technology to old workflows and organizational arrangements and by using pieces of the old and new technology side by side. Historical examples abound. For example, horse-powered vehicles and farm implements operated alongside trucks and tractors on farms, and multistoried factories (relics of early belt-utilizing steam or electric technologies) were converted to utilize more modern beltless electric motors. This third generalization is of major importance as we examine the current applications of computerization in organizations. What we find in practice is likely to be only a partial adoption—an accommodation to modernization effected by melding the new and old technologies. This accommodation often gives rise to paper-driven systems in which computers provide new levels of efficiency but are underutilized in terms of state-of-the art efficiency or range of applications.

Taken together, these generalizations provide insight and a perspective from which to examine the evidence. On the one hand, we need to understand how technological advances drive organizational change and how evolving perceptions, aptitudes, and expectations, particularly those associated with a generational changing-of-the-guard in management and labor, bring pressures for adoption. On the other, we need to assess the financial, cultural, and organizational factors that inhibit change. Finally, we must recognize the role of adaptation and be sensitive to the fact that observed practices frequently represent compromises between the old and the new that in time must give way to more effective applications.

The implication of these three generalizations is that any inquiry into the impact of computer technology on labor—especially if it is concerned with the pace at which change is taking place and is likely to take place in the years immediately ahead—must assess both positive and negative factors. Moreover, such an inquiry must recognize that the forces at work act not only in a direct fashion, that is, through changing work assignments as the new technology is applied to the existing set of operations. They also work indirectly through complex processes of diffusion involving, among other things, changes in organizational arrangements and changes in missions performed. (Some applications pertain to a wide range of functions within departments of the user firm or institution, and others make possible new final services or products.)

Some Highlights of Three Decades
of General Process Computer Usage

If current organizational practices and plans relating to computerization reflect technological changes in the past and managerial adaptation to these changes, it is important as a first step in analysis to examine quickly the history of past changes in computer technology, at least as they relate to administrative applications. In the following discussion I highlight the principal developments of the period extending from roughly the late 1950s to the 1980s, describing some key characteristics of several of the most widely used earlier computers, the IBM 650, 1401, 360, and 370 series, as well as certain developments in related technologies since the beginning of the 1970s.

The First and Second Generations of Computers

The first generation, which made use of banks of vacuum tubes instead of the modern-day integrated circuits contained on silicon chips, was invented in 1947, but the technology did not find its way into general administrative, governmental, and business usage until the advent of the IBM 650 almost a decade later (1955). Rapid growth followed, and several first-generation computers were introduced. An old-time computer salesman reminiscing to the author about the IBM 650 recalled that "they expected a sale of about 20 but sold over 2,000 the first year."

Nevertheless, commercial application was in its infancy in the early 1960s when the IBM 1401, the most popular of the second-generation computers (using transistors rather than vacuum tubes), was introduced. It was widely utilized for general-purpose office work, especially accounting, and in the processing of payroll, personnel, and inventory records. The 1401, like the more primitive 650 before it, was designed for use principally with keypunched cards, which converted data into electrical, digital signals.[2] The computer was equipped with only a limited internal processing system (about the same capacity as a small microprocessor today) and performed only one task at a time. Operation was time consuming and difficult; cards provided instructions (the "program"), and cards contained basic data introduced in sequence. Each updating or alteration of the data required that new cards be punched and introduced into the data set through resorting. Information derived from one set of computations (e.g., payroll) could be introduced into another (e.g., accounting) only by using the output cards of the first as an input to the second.

The system was totally paper driven; data were entered first onto forms and transcribed to cards by the keypunch operator.[3] Processing was sequential (each batch of cards was processed in its proper order) and subject to interruptions (e.g., accounting runs could not begin until payroll and other necessary computations had been made). Because data were stored on cards and not in the memory of the machine or on disks, awkward and time-consuming resorting was necessary to update data sets with each new processing operation.

Yet the new technology was extremely useful in saving clerical labor where large bodies of data were processed. Rosters could be updated or originated (e.g., employees' names along with other information could be sorted according to any criterion for which information could be coded). Information obtained for one department could be transferred to another without laborious clerical transcription. Computations were uniformly accurate, and with properly coded instructions the computer could perform a variety of complex manipulations of the data. For example, payroll computations could be made independently for each employee that recognized differences in salary, hours worked, marital and tax status, and other deductions.

The Third Generation of Computers: The IBM 360

The third generation of computers (utilizing integrated circuits) brought major advances in the late 1960s. Among the first of these computers was the IBM 360. It was equipped with a built-in input/output control system that made it possible to access disks or tapes to bring data into the memory system. It was no longer necessary for the operator to position data in the old sequential way because the machine could be instructed through the program to retrieve information as needed. Moreover, these computers were capable of multiprocessing; many runs could be carried out simultaneously, and as a result, work programs did not have to wait one upon the other. In addition, the new computers could accept information simultaneously from multiple channels. Terminals could be operated in a number of locations for on-line operations, although hardwiring (i.e., special lines) was required, and transmission distances were limited. Data retrieval was also possible but largely in a simple preprogrammed form.

But in spite of these advances data processing operations still required a large amount of clerical preparation. Data were typically set down on paper, keypunched, and batch processed.[4] Moreover, most information derived from the computer was departmentally oriented. Reports were periodic, issued in printout form, and designed by the computer center in a fixed format. Ad hoc reports were available only with delay and, for the most part, only at the request of higher-level executives.

The New Technology of the 1970s and 1980s

It is interesting that there is no recognized fourth generation of computers, although the Japanese have dubbed the supercomputers that they are currently developing for artificial intelligence work as "fifth generation." Since the early third-generation models were introduced, computers have developed rapidly, incorporating a number of major improvements.

The IBM 370 may be regarded as representative of the modern computers that came into use in the early 1970s. It brought dramatic advances in computational power and development of on-line capabilities with a wide range of new applications. Increased computational capability was made possible through radically new software design, the development of microchips, and major advances in hardware design that made possible different modes of computing ("virtual systems") whereby disk-stored information became an integral and instantaneously accessed part of the computer memory (instead of stored data read into the internal memory). As a result, memory became, for all practical purposes, unlimited.

Such access coupled with the increased capability for multiprocessing in turn made possible the retrieval and processing of information from different parts of the memory system. A computer could access, for example, a variety of information for a single employee such as home address, age, employment and payroll records, and vacation and sick leave experience, and could summarize or process further any and all such information.

At the same time, the new technology introduced modern on-line data processing capability utilizing the telephone and other telecommunications systems.[5] Access to the computer for entry, retrieval, and statistical reporting was no longer restricted to the computer center but began to pass outward to the user.

Since the advent of the IBM 370 and similar computers by other vendors, there have been major advances on a broad front: the continued development of large computers; major breakthroughs in telecommunications, including the development and installation of satellite, microwave, cable, and optical fiber transmission systems and a variety of electronic switching hardware to facilitate on-line computer usage; major advances in both the theory and practice of software engineering; the introduction of powerful but less expensive minicomputers for use in industrial and scientific applications and in smaller administrative systems; radical innovations and improvements in peripheral equipment; and, most recently, the introduction of the microcomputer, or personal computer, and the development of the supercomputer.

The personal computer (PC) deserves special attention for in a sense it brings with it a new set of applications and opportunities. As one veteran management information systems (MIS) executive explained to the author, "It's an anomaly. On one hand, it's a glorified desk calculator. On the other, it's a chunk of the big computer on your desk with an extended umbilical cord." At least three features distinguish the personal computer from its predecessors: a high level of computational capability at a very low price;[6] capability for both stand-alone and on-line operation coupled with availability of add-on disk pack storage and high speed printers; and a new variety of easy-to-use and versatile software.

The latter is particularly significant. Designed for business, professional, and recreational use in the office and in the home, the new computer opened up a broad and lucrative market for a new type of software designed for the nontechnical user. The effect has been a spawning of what is essentially a new "industry," one that literally produces thousands of programs that enable the operator to utilize the computer (with relatively little instruction) for a wide array of applications ranging from games, word processing, and electronic mail to cash management and spread-sheet analysis.

In addition, the capability for both stand-alone and on-line operation, coupled with add-on disk pack storage and high speed printing, increases enormously the versatility of the PC. In the stand-alone mode, the PC can be utilized for a variety of statistical analyses as well as for word processing and filing of information in both written and data form. Of special importance is the fact that the PC, particularly when augmented by additional storage, can be used to computerize special activities within an organization without waiting for the often lengthy processes of planning, software preparation, and installation of large mainframes or minicomputer systems. Applications such as cash management, scheduling, and budgeting are becoming increasingly common. In many instances the data base is accumulated within the given activity center, but the range of applications can be readily broadened simply by utilizing disks upon which information has been transferred from the main computer or elsewhere.

Alternatively, the microcomputer can be linked to larger systems to operate on line as a terminal for entry and retrieval of information, for communication, or for use as a processing center that can be "uploaded" with data for processing or "downloaded" to transfer the processed output to computers elsewhere in the system.

The most recent development in computer technologies involves the building of supercomputers. The Cyber 205 at the Princeton Forrestal Center provides an example of such a computer, of which there are at least 150 in operation around the world. It is linked to the twelve-member Consortium for Scientific Computing that includes Princeton, the Institute for Advanced Study, and ten other universities and has the computational speed of roughly 7,500 IBM PCs.[7] In 1987, the Cyber 205 will be replaced by the ETA 10, a machine twenty times as powerful. These supercomputers make use of parallel computing and other advances in computer architecture and are characterized by enormous memory capacity as well as computational speed. The ETA 10 will have a memory capacity comparable to the entire holdings of the Library of Congress.[8]

A New Era of Technology

This brief review of the evolution of computer and related technology not only indicates the remarkable achievements of the past three decades and conveys some sense of the broad range of applications that has been opened up, but also supports an observation of central importance: The advances that have occurred, although cumulative and evolutionary in nature, must be seen for analytical purposes as falling into two stages. The first, which embraces first-, second-, and third-generation computing, was characterized largely by basic "back-office" applications, which although effective in increasing the productivity of clerical labor and providing useful new information to management, involved large amounts of paperwork. Moreover, there were severe restrictions on the extent to which information could be shared by different agencies or departments within a large organization or could be processed to provide effective control or planning data for middle and upper management.

The second stage, which began in the mid-1970s and is still evolving rapidly, must be regarded as a significantly different era. What distinguishes it most clearly from the earlier stage is the application of on-line processing (the joining of computer and telecommunications technology) coupled with quite revolutionary advances that permit virtually unlimited storage and access to data. Together, these advances make it possible for organizations to build integrated data-base systems with distributed processing capability. These new-era systems are integrated in the sense that information subsystems within the organization are tied together through telecommunications to share access to data bases into which information can be entered and stored or from which data can be retrieved. The capability for distributed processing means that individuals may process data at terminals or microcomputers located at their own workplaces rather than relying upon the central data processing unit to perform such operations. Moreover, in these new-era systems, the range of computer operations has been extended to encompass a much broader array of activities and to make possible new organizational arrangements under which management is provided with quantitatively and qualitatively greater amounts of information.

Major Implications of New-Era Computerization for Work and Organizational Structure

The distinction between first- and second-stage computerization provides a basis for judging how far organizations have progressed in applying modern technology.[9] Today the use of computers for administrative data processing is widespread. Virtually all large organizations, both public and private, own and operate large computers; and the majority of medium-sized firms as well as many smaller firms utilize electronic data processing (EDP) in a variety of operations, typically with their own hardware (although many make at least some use of data processing services). This widespread popularity of computerization and the advances that have been made in productivity tend to obscure the fact that most data processing has not yet moved into the second stage. Even when fairly modern computers are installed, EDP is most often performed in the old-time, paper-driven batch mode (even where terminals are used for data entry) and is restricted in its range of applications. Systems are seldom integrated, and modern, fully distributed processing is rarer still because it requires both on-line data-base systems and considerable change in work organization.

Yet our society is moving inexorably toward widespread adoption of new-era technology, and its adoption is bringing about major changes in work and organization. Some sectors (particularly banking and insurance) and some large, progressive firms in otherwise fairly backward sectors have already made major advances. The task for research is twofold: to distinguish new- from old-era operations and observe where and how rapidly the adoption of the new is taking place; and to observe the impact on work of the emergent technology across a number of sectors and a number of different types of organizations.

Regarding the latter, both businesses and nonprofit organizations are likely to vary widely in terms of the products and services they produce. Accordingly, the impact of new-era technology on work may be expected to vary even though there may be a number of activities performed in a similar manner. What we must seek is an understanding of both differences and similarities—a knowledge upon which can be based generalizations as to this technology's effect on the way men and women everywhere earn a living and on the kind of public policy such an effect necessitates.

Reduction of Low-Level Clerical Work

The highly developed capabilities of the modern computer for multiprocessing, multiple access and retrieval, and massive information storage make possible information processing systems that possess a remarkable characteristic: Information can be entered into the computer memory once and stored along with other information to generate a data base. Thereafter it can be accessed and subjected to processing, augmented by adding other related information, or brought together with information from other computer memories (i.e., other data bases) for inspection or statistical manipulation.

This ability to build and utilize data bases stands at the heart of new-era computer applications and has major implications for the future of low-level clerical work. It means that laborious entry of information onto paper can be sharply reduced or even eliminated. Basic information is entered directly into the computer and can be retrieved, summed with other data, sorted, or analyzed statistically without being transposed to worksheets; where "hard copy" is required, this information can be produced in printed form upon instruction. Thus, old-time, low-level clerical work (recording information on paper, checking for transposition and computational errors, filing, and myriad routine tasks inherent in paper-driven offices) is sharply reduced.

To be sure, documents and reports continue to abound in administrative systems that are substantially computerized, but such paper tends to fall into one of three groups, each of which will become less important as the new technology is utilized more completely. The first group includes documents that constitute evidence of responsibility or obligation (e.g., orders, documents of certification, contracts) and that validate or authorize information entered into computer systems. At present, such paper is an integral part of the administrative system, and often passes from office to office where it is filed and refiled. Yet new technology is available that permits transmission and computer filing of the image of a document; still other technology makes possible the validation of computer-processed information by special coding. Thus, the way is open for major reductions in the reliance on such paper in the years immediately ahead, although as yet very little reduction has occurred.

The second group comprises correspondence, which, as one leading MIS consultant has noted, is for the most part generated internally (as much as 90 percent) in large organizations. The adoption of electronic mail will eliminate an important share of such paper processing, but this technology is not yet widely utilized.[10]

The third encompasses computer printouts. Today's office is likely to be equipped with a large number of filing cabinets bulging with computer-generated reports and analyses. Frequently, the particular information desired by the administrator must be extracted by a clerk and submitted in memo form or processed further using a desk calculator. As distributed processing that utilizes PCs or other terminals comes increasingly into use, hard copy stored in printout form will play a less important role.

Reduction of Middle-Level
Clerical-Administrative Work

The capability of modern computerization is not, however, restricted to eliminating tasks formerly performed by low-level clerical personnel but, rather, embraces a wide range of computational tasks. Under earlier arrangements it was necessary to assemble large amounts of information, perform calculations and prepare statistical summaries, accounting, inventory, and purchasing reports, budget estimates, labor utilization schedules, and the like. Such work was performed by a variety of clerical and lower managerial personnel who through long experience and on-the-job training acquired considerable specialized knowledge. Moreover, such work performed under these arrangements gave the individual in charge monopolistic power over information. Information was available only from the person who was in charge of putting together the given data. Higher management consulted that person and that person alone when additional information was needed.

Although earlier computerization did away with a variety of tedious, repetitive hand calculations, modern technology makes it possible to program entire complex processing operations by drawing on information within the data base to produce reports, schedules, and so on; likewise, ready access to processed information in a variety of formats is also available. The result is that old work assignments are eliminated and old skills that required years of experience and training may no longer be of value. With the most modern systems, information is readily available from any clerk at the terminal or is directly accessible to the upper-level manager if his or her desk is equipped with a microcomputer.

New Tasks and Modes of Work

If data-base systems reduce the need for much old-style clerical and lower-level managerial work, what new tasks and new modes of work are introduced? The answer lies in the very nature of the technological transformation that is occurring and in the kind of information processing that the new era of technology engenders.

Information processing for administrative purposes may be divided into three general categories: operational, control, and strategic. With precomputer systems most human effort was devoted to the preparation and manipulation of operational information—which included payroll, accounts receivable and billing, personnel records, the processing of purchases, and other similar functions. Information processing for managerial control (such as budgeting, inventory, cash management, and the like) received less attention and was carried out through rudimentary systems. Strategic information processing for planning and mapping strategies was allocated the least resources and was dependent on relatively limited and hard-to-secure information.

In short, early precomputer information processing can be visualized as a pyramid with the large base representing operational-type information processing, a much smaller middle portion, decision-support information processing, and the very small upper portion at the apex, strategic information. The allocation of work—human effort—involved in information processing could be represented in a similar fashion.

Old-era computerization altered the structure significantly by abridging the amount of work required at all levels but principally at the lowest operational level, while increasing the amount of information at all levels. New-era computerization introduces more dramatic changes.[11] A much larger amount of information can be processed at all levels, especially at the decision control and strategic levels, but even more dramatic changes are possible in terms of work. The lowest level of operational processing is largely taken over by the computer; much of the data handling and filing becomes computerized. Lower-level clerical tasks are altered. Many positions are eliminated or combined—the clerk increasingly is assigned to a terminal at a workstation and is made responsible for entering and retrieving data and for instructing the computer regarding the information to be processed.

Although tasks are simplified by "friendly" programming, the operator must cope with a larger volume of information. Frequently, although not always, the information processed relates to a broader range of activities and thereby requires that the operator develop a clearer understanding of how the department and, indeed, the overall organization function.

At the higher clerical levels and lower managerial levels the older complex computational tasks give way to new work. With information readily available these middle personnel, who now are freed from manual data handling (and in some instances supervisory) chores, can be assigned new roles—to make sales or handle customer complaints, to analyze operations and take over additional administrative responsibilities in the department, or to perform entirely new functions not previously feasible. A considerable reshuffling of work and responsibility is possible according to the special needs and responsibilities of the organization, but the general thrust of change is likely to be toward increasing the scope and level of responsibility of clerical and middle-level managerial personnel.

As for upper management, increased access to key information pertaining to every facet of operations coupled with the ability to pose "what if" questions, to make projections, and to raise the level of strategic analysis are likely to shift the focus of this level's work and to increase its effectiveness.

Changing Workflows and Organizational Structures

But the impact of changing computer technology cannot be understood without recognizing the role of reorganization in changing workflows, job content, and responsibilities. From the outset, adoption of computer technology has required organizational change. In the 1960s and 1970s, organizations were altered to establish computer centers, which became the focal points for computational work and preparation of reports. Basic data were fed to computer centers by user departments that for the most part retained their earlier organizational structures, although internal arrangements were often changed somewhat to reflect the changing needs brought about by new computer applications.

With the advent of complex new-era systems, pressure for organizational changes arises. The logic of integrated, on-line systems requires new structures to accommodate changed flows of work and allocations of staff. For example, the old arrangements under which extensive preparation of both payroll and personnel records might justify separate departments give way to work patterns that may call into question the divisions of responsibility if not the need for separate organizational entities. At the same time, distributed processing tends to shift the locus of both routine computing and report preparation outward to the user agency and to bring about an emphasis on data analysis for managerial control and planning. Organizational change is therefore a concomitant, and often a prerequisite, of computerization and frequently contributes to redefinitions of work assignments and the creation of new job hierarchies.

Some Key Characteristics of Nonprofit Organizations

Although municipal governments, universities, and hospitals perform very different missions and differ in countless ways, they share certain fundamental characteristics that make it appropriate to group them in a study of the impact of computerization on work.

1. They are large service organizations. Their output is a variety of "products" that are unstandardized in character and involve many "transactions."

2. Their operations are labor intensive. These industries, in contrast to manufacturing and agriculture, do not have a long history of labor-saving technology.[12]

3. They are complex organizations (in part a corollary to number 1) comprising a number of loosely knit departments or agencies with relatively weak top-down control.

4. For the most part, their operations have been characterized by lax and unsophisticated approaches to cost accounting, cost control, and revenue gathering. Typically, little effort has been made in the past to determine specific service costs or to identify areas of low productivity. Where pricing arrangements are employed, little attention has been given to the cost of services rendered or to the sensitivity of demand to price changes.[13] Behind this general laxness in attention to financial management lie a number of factors; one of the most important has been the availability of important alternative sources of revenue (alternatives to taxes in cities and to tuition and fees in universities and hospitals). Cities have been able to look to state and federal governments for important revenue and universities to governmental and foundation grants and to alumni contributions. Hospitals have benefited from foundation and governmental grants and, where fees are charged, have been largely insulated from market pressures by methods of third-party (e.g., Blue Cross and Blue Shield Associations) remuneration in which historical costs have, until the recent advent of prospective payment arrangements, been covered virtually without question.

5. A fifth shared characteristic follows at least in part from the first four. Each group of institutions is currently under extreme pressure to contain costs and to increase productivity. Each is facing financial crises; most individual organizations are critically in need of tighter organization, closer cost control, and more informed planning.

Thus, for reasons stemming from a combination of these characteristics, there is logic in studying in the same context the efforts of city governments, hospitals, and universities and colleges to introduce modern computer-telecommunications and related technology. It is the task of the following chapters to examine the extent to which these organizations are adopting the new technology and the impact of these efforts on work and employment opportunity.

Notes

1. Alvin Toffler, *The Third Wave* (New York: William Morrow and Co., Inc., 1980).

2. Keypunching was already a well-established technique for transcribing data because it had been used in the electrical accounting machine (EAM) technology that preceded electronic computers. It has been estimated that in 1954 the U.S. government employed 5,000 keypunch operators to prepare data for its accounting and tabulating machines (nonelectronic).

3. Other devices could be used to provide data inputs to these first-generation computers, but keypunching was the principal method. Punched tape and magnetic tapes were alternative modes, but these could not be altered to accept new data, as was possible with cards.

4. The number of keypunchers and verifiers in use in the United States did not begin to decline until the 1970s.

5. Remote data processing utilizing terminals and telecommunications originated in 1958 when the first airline reservation system was installed. Airline systems were followed by stock quotation systems in the early 1960s. These systems were very large and costly, however, and were not available to the general user.

6. An MIS executive interviewed by the author pointed to the personal computer on his desk and said, "That PC cost $2500 and can handle 380,000 memory units. The IBM machine I used in 1971 cost $800,000 and could handle 246,000."

7. J. I. Merritt, "Approaches to Supercomputing," *Princeton Alumni Weekly*, 86, 7, Dec. 4, 1985, pp. 17-18.

8. Ibid., p. 18.

9. The following discussion of the impact of the new-era technology on work deals only with employers who are principally engaged in processing and using information. It does not deal with production-type jobs or scientific and engineering work.

10. One information service official in the New York City government remarked to the author, "Look at this desk, loaded down with paper—and in an *MIS* office. Yet every piece is necessary. Each is a formal request for new hardware from one agency or another. We're a long way from the paperless office."

11. The descriptions of work changes with new era technology are based on the findings of Thierry Noyelle in his studies of banking and insurance and on

my own interviews of large corporations in department store retailing and in food manufacturing and distribution (firms that are well advanced in the use of best-practice systems). See Thierry Noyelle, *Beyond Industrial Dualism: Market and Job Segmentation in the New Economy* (Boulder, Colo.: Westview, 1987).

12. The remarkable advances in medical technology of the postwar period do not contradict this generalization because these advances had as their focus the provision of new methods of diagnosis and treatment; these advances were not for the purpose of increasing labor productivity.

13. Cities have tended to show a similar unwillingness to analyze the underlying forces of demand in tax administration.

2

Computerization in the Public Sector: The New York City Experience

The New York City government is one of the largest organizations in the United States, with a budget of $21.5 billion and employment of roughly 330,000 persons of which 140,000 are within the mayoral agencies. Size alone would suggest a major need for application of computer technology to assist in administration, but that need is compounded by the nature of the city's organization and operations. The New York City government is complex and comprises eighteen major mayoral agencies and six major nonmayoral agencies or authorities (including the Board of Education and the Health and Hospitals Corporation, or HHC), each with a number of departments or subagencies.

But size, complexity, and range of activities alone do not make the city (and by extension other major municipal governments as well) a prime candidate for application of computer and related technologies. The special nature of city government is a significant qualifying factor. Most agencies continually perform a vast number of individual tasks as they carry out their assigned roles of delivering services to individuals and businesses and collecting tax revenues. Coping with these myriad tasks requires a tremendous amount of recordkeeping, monitoring, tracking, planning, and analyses.

Richard Davidoff, head of the city's Office of Computer Plans and Controls (OCPC), has suggested that modern computer systems designed to cope with the vast array of activities carried out by city governments are of four general types:[1]

1. Recordkeeping, general administration, managerial control systems. Examples: payroll, personnel records, general accounting, accounts payable, budgetary control, tax assessment and collection.
2. Dispatching-scheduling systems. Examples: the 911 Police Department system, the Starfire Fire Department alarm-dispatching

system, emergency ambulance dispatch, garbage collection, street cleaning, and snow removal.
3. Complaint systems. Examples: streetlight complaints, tenant heating complaints, air pollution complaints.
4. Tracking-monitoring systems. Examples: tracking summons and scofflaw records by the Parking Violations Bureau, determining eligibility and following up the disposition of welfare cases, tracking cases through the courts.

It is readily apparent that a host of city government responsibilities are readily grouped under Davidoff's classification schema. At present, many activities are directly or indirectly computer assisted; many are not. In either event, the case for New York City as a major candidate for computerization seems indisputable.

The Push to Computerize

Although the earlier history of computer applications in New York City government was relatively restricted and unprogressive,[2] the period beginning, roughly, in 1978 has seen the city move rapidly into an era of widespread computerization and utilization of modern equipment in a broad array of applications. As shown below, these new applications have resulted in significant savings, generated substantial revenues, and improved the quality of services rendered.

In large measure the new push to computerize the city's administration may be regarded as an outgrowth of the fiscal crisis.[3] As a result of the extreme pressure generated by the budget crisis, a number of developments took place that contributed significantly to the new era of computerization. An oversight agency, the Office of Computer Plans and Controls (OCPC), was established, as was a major city computer services bureau, the Computer Services Center (CSC). Mandates for reform by the State of New York and the federal government, which were associated with new finance arrangements and revision of the city's charter, helped create the city's Integrated Financial Management System (IFMS). Under IFMS, the Financial Information Services Agency (FISA) was established to track the budgets of the city's 120 bureaus and agencies in order to facilitate accounting and management control and to provide modern computer processing of payroll and purchase orders. Finally, the Productivity Council was created as a mandate of the Federal Loan Guarantee Act of 1978 to bring together high-level agency and labor representatives to develop projects for increasing productivity (including computerization as well as other initiatives) and to work for management and labor cooperation in carrying through these initiatives.

Each of these developments led to an advance in computerizing the city's government. OCPC, organized within the mayor's office, has become a clearing agency for approving equipment purchases (to assure compatibility of equipment and economic allocation of resources) and for developing new computerization projects. It is also the key agency for long-term planning to bring about continued modernization and a higher level of interagency coordination. A recent achievement has been the development (in conjunction with the Office of Telecommunications Control) of CITYNET, a citywide data communications network, which is expected to cut costs by more than $40 million during the first five years of operation by rationalizing the use of leased communications facilities.

CSC, formed in 1979, operates within the Department of General Services and is one of the six mayoral agencies that maintain large centralized multifunctional computer installations.[4] It operates computing facilities utilized by more than seventy agencies and provides support for computerization in both small and large agencies. Agencies that have no hardware may come to CSC for hardware resources, although the responsibility for the development of the applications programs lies with the agencies.

FISA operates a large computer center and employs a staff of experienced computer specialists, many recruited from industry. It has made a major contribution toward cost cutting and increased efficiency by subjecting the expenditures of city bureaus and agencies to tightened budgetary control and by providing an important element for citywide procurement and payroll management.

The Productivity Council with its Labor-Management Committee is not only active in proposing areas for possible productivity increases but has been a key factor in sparking the interest and acceptance necessary for bringing about new applications. Its unique contribution has been to bring management and labor together as equal partners in the process of seeking new areas for increased productivity and in paving the way for acceptance of computerization.

But OCPC, CPS, FISA, and the Productivity Council are by no means the only factors responsible for pushing the city toward modernization. In spite of continued budget stringency, the city has found the money to develop and implement a multiplicity of new projects. This push culminated in a budget of $250 million for computerization in fiscal 1984.[5]

Improvements in Productivity and Service

The range and variety of efforts to bring computer technology to the city's administration are difficult to convey in brief compass, but some sense of the extent of accomplishment can be gained from *The Mayor's Management Report*, of September 1984 (see Appendix A). Other essential aspects of the New York City experience that were brought out in interviews in the Mayor's Office of Operations and in a number of the major agencies.[6] At least five of these aspects are critical to an understanding of what has occurred within the city since the late 1970s.

The move to modern systems. The move to computerize has been an effort not simply to broaden the scope of applications but to modernize the system from top to bottom. Several of the city's major computer systems now operate largely on line. Even where batch processing based on data entered on paper forms is still utilized, on-line entry and retrieval are commonplace. (CSC also maintains a center in the Municipal Building where data entry for batch processing can be carried out by agencies that do not yet have on-line capability.)

It was repeatedly brought home to this investigator that potentialities of computer technology can be realized only when modern equipment and sophisticated software are utilized. This applies, for example, in the Human Resources Administration (HRA) where the individual records of 918,000 public assistance recipients are continuously updated and can be instantly monitored at 1,120 terminals located in forty income maintenance centers throughout the city; and in the capability of the Finance Department to provide rapid and accurate information to taxpayers on the status of assessment and payments and to ferret out individuals and corporations for noncompliance. It also obtains in the new capability of the city to examine its aging infrastructure, to move systematically toward effective maintenance and renewal, to monitor its vast array of contractors, and to keep track of the thousands of complaints regarding heating, traffic signs, and streetlights.

In short, the city's experience demonstrates how modern computer technology utilizing telecommunications and newly developed hardware and software opens up new vistas for the management of large organizations, increases the range and quality of services, reduces the unit costs of services performed, and improves planning and control.

Financial feasibility. New computer systems are largely cost effective. Although it is true that the city's budgetary mandates have favored expenditures for hardware, software, and outside services over increases in payroll (personnel is separately and more stringently controlled), new computerization projects are subject to sharp scrutiny. Only because the array of new initiatives were proven cost effective and/or shown to result in significant improvement in services was money found for the city's aggressive push to modernize.[7] Evidence of significant savings will be found in many of the applications discussed in Appendix A. The lesson for public sector organizations, and private sector firms as well, is that budgetary considerations are not likely to long delay initiatives in computerization once a major effort to modernize has been mounted.

Development of supporting systems. In most of the operational agencies interviewed (HRA, Finance Department, Police Department, Sanitation Department, Personnel Department), it was found that computerization, far from being limited to a handful of major applications related to key activities, was utilized for a number of administrative, operational, and planning tasks. In HRA, for example, systems were utilized to monitor, schedule, and plan in areas such as procurement, operation and maintenance of the 350 buildings under its care, security, office management, and personnel management. In the Police Department, applications were extending far beyond the 911 and squad car dispatching systems to a variety of activities including fingerprint analysis, arrest procedures, personnel records, and daily scheduling of police.

Word processing is widely utilized and has become for many agencies the principal mode for processing correspondence and documents. As of late 1984, there were more than 1,000 word processor workstations with a number equipped as microcomputers for electronic mail handling and other uses.[8]

Of special interest is the city's experience to date with personal computers. Several years ago the Mayor's Office of Operations aggressively pushed the use of PCs by placing them in a number of agencies and encouraging middle management to experiment with possible applications. Every agency interviewed was utilizing these versatile and inexpensive computers, had ordered more, and was planning for extended use. Nevertheless, the number of personal computers in actual use remains small and probably totaled no more than several hundred in early 1985. Several agencies reported that they were experiencing delays of a year or more in securing approval and expressed considerable dismay and frustration.

Organizational resistance versus the contagiousness of computing. It must be recognized that because the interviewees were principally managers who were deeply involved in the computerization effort and were enthusiastic regarding their accomplishments, there was probably a degree of favorable bias in their remarks. Administrators interviewed in the Mayor's Office of Operations, the Labor Management Committee Program, and OCPC—those in a position to observe the overall experience— admitted freely that progress had been very uneven. Some agencies, they noted, had been reluctant to push computerization and were proceeding slowly, and even within the more progressive agencies some applications were still paper oriented. It was agreed that, taken as a whole, the massive bureaucracy of New York City still has a long way to go before it is completely modernized.

Yet everywhere there was evidence of a growing momentum—a new "contagiousness" that was transforming resistance into enthusiasm. The Sanitation Department is a clear example. It was reported by the top MIS executive that all levels of the organization had eagerly sought the new SCAN network system (a modern integrated reporting and scheduling network for garbage collection and snow removal in the five boroughs) not only because it made administration of the system easier and more effective, but also because it brought prestige to the organization. To work with a modern state-of-the-art computer system added luster to the department as it compared itself to the other uniformed services (police and fire).

Indirect contributions of computerization. Thus far I have considered only the direct effects of computerization on cost reduction and efficiency, but there are innumerable indirect contributions as well. *The Mayor's Management Report* observed that the amount in savings and revenue captured from all productivity projects in the ongoing Program to Eliminate the Gap was $138 million in fiscal 1983 and an additional $180 million in fiscal 1984.[9] Only a part of this increased productivity can be directly attributable to computerization. Other initiatives are documented in the report under a number of headings including "Managing the City's Work Force" (examples: managing overtime, reducing absences, devising alternative work schedules, reducing costs by using two-member sanitation crews, increasing civilianization in the Police Department, replacing per diem nurses); "Improving Work Methods" (examples: ensuring that all personnel have the parts and tools to do their jobs well, improving pothole identification, reducing HRA errors and overpayment); "Capital Investment and Technological Improvements" (examples: reducing drafting and design time, providing firefighters with automatic descriptions of any hazardous conditions near a reported fire, reducing the downtime of automatic paving machines); "Risk Management" (examples: decreasing cost of tort settlement through analysis of past experience and cost of litigation through tracking and expansion of the document control system); "Audit Implementation" (examples: audits to improve coordination between Departments of Sanitation and Police in removing abandoned vehicles, city audit to improve inventory and warehousing controls, audits of energy conservation efforts, Aid to Families wih Dependent Children payments, *in rem* property rent collection); and "Quality of Life Enforcement" (examples: a variety of efforts to reduce traffic fatalities, improve traffic flow, and enforce environmental protection codes).

Among these many initiatives, we see the combined effects of changed work organization, applications of technology other than computers, new training programs, and application of new computer systems. Few if any of these efforts would have been successful, or successful to the same degree, without the availability of computer technology. In many instances the computer's role is central; in many, it is indirect. In virtually all instances it is significant because computerization permits management to locate trouble spots and measure accomplishment.

Four Data Systems at Closer Range

The following brief descriptions of four major systems provide a closer look at what takes place with the adoption of modern computerization than can be gained from the preceding general discussion. The descriptions illustrate certain capabilities of modern computer systems; demonstrate how modern systems can be tied in with less modern systems when complete stem-to-stern revamping is not feasible; provide some indication of the magnitude of the training required; and call attention to the need for reorganization inherent in the changing rearrangement of workflows and administrative responsibility brought about by the new systems.

New York City's Integrated Financial
Management System (IFMS)

IFMS was installed on July 1, 1977, and it was the first major on-line system to be completed after the city's financial crisis. From the outset it influenced every agency in the city by radically revising financial reporting and monitoring systems to improve control, planning, analysis, and accountability. By bringing modern on-line technology to the agencies, IFMS familiarized both management and clerical staff with the system's use and potentialities.

IFMS was designed to provide the machinery for rigorous budgetary control and careful managerial practice previously lacking in the city by integrating four major subsystems: budgeting, accounting, payroll, and purchasing. IFMS does not provide for preparation of payrolls but receives the prepared payroll information, monitors for budgetary appropriateness, and prepares checks for payment. In purchasing, the system receives requisitions and contract proposals, encumbers funds to ensure that no purchasing commitments are made unless sufficient funds are available, and subsequently approves payment upon confirmation of the purchase and makes final payment. All financial information becomes simultaneously available to the accounting and budgetary offices, which in turn perform their respective functions and provide reports and information. IFMS has radically altered the city's financial management system by:[10]

1. providing a unified financial management system. Before IFMS, financial management was fragmented among a number of systems involving several data processing facilities. Moreover, budgetary expenditure totals from different systems were incompatible and required difficult reconciliation. Under IFMS, however,

> Citywide budgeting, accounting, purchasing, and payroll functions are brought together in a single computer facility . . . FISA. In the IFMS computer system each major subsystem (such as Payroll) is able to access data from a single data base that also holds information from the other subsystems (such as Budget) . . . IFMS is unified in another important respect—account coding in the Budget and Accounting subsystems is identical, greatly simplifying agency coding on vouchers and comparisons of budgeted to actual performances.

2. defining centers of budgetary responsibility. Under IFMS, agencies are required to budget by "responsibility centers."

> Responsibility centers are units that are part of an agency's organizational hierarchy and are under the control of a specific manager. Thus, every budgeted revenue dollar is associated with a responsibility center and a designated manager responsible for monitoring expenditures and revenues. Organizational arrangements long used to structure agency operations— police precincts, district health offices, fire, and sanitation borough commands—appear for the first time in the budget.

3. preparing monthly plans. Although the annual budget remains the primary financial control instrument for spending and revenues, agencies are now required to prepare monthly plans for expenditures (or budgetary incumbrances) and for revenues. IFMS prepares monthly reports in turn and thereby provides comparisons of monthly activity to plans and to annual forecasts.

Clearly IFMS has had important effects on both organization and work in both the central agencies of the system (the Office of Management and Budget [OMB], the Office of the Comptroller, and the Finance Department) and the city's line agencies. According to *An Introduction to IFMS*, the number of staff members extensively affected in terms of work and responsibilities were as shown in Table 2.1.

TABLE 2.1
Number of Employees Affected by IFMS

Agency	Employees
Central agencies	
Office of Management and Budget	275
Comptroller	800
Finance Department	150
Line agencies	
Managerial, professional, and clerical Staff in IFMS functional areas	
Budget and fiscal officer and staff	500
Accounting and auditing staff	500
Purchasing staff	1,000
Payroll staff	600
Center managers (not including staff)	1,200
	5,025

Source: The Urban Academy, *An Introduction to IFMS*, 2nd ed., New York, December 1977, pp. 107–112.

Given the extent to which work was reorganized and redefined and personnel was affected, the requirements for training were extensive. The task of training for the revised work assignments was primarily the responsibility of the Urban Academy, which directed its efforts to several major areas: overview training (for personnel in OMB and the Comptroller's Office, executive and senior managers in the line agencies, and personnel requiring special financial system training); financial management training (in functional and technical skills required by financial managers to make IFMS effective); and procedural (supervisory and clerical) training (including special training for input procedures, application workshops, and maintenance training). During the period from July 1976 to July 1977 alone, IFMS training was provided to more than 6,000 city personnel in more than 38,000 contact hours—an average of slightly more than one full day per person.[11]

The preceding discussion of IFMS is summary in nature, but it does provide an indication of the extent to which introduction of a major integrated management system brings about top-to-bottom changes in the organization of work and responsibilities; it also suggests the comprehensive nature of the training effort necessary to implement such a system. No detailed evidence was gathered through interviews regarding the number of transfers, promotions, discharges, or new hires that resulted from the institution of IFMS, but it must be emphasized that the entire program of system design and introduction was carried out within the framework of civil service regulations and union contract protection, which ensure that workers will not be discharged as a result of organizational changes or redefinition of work content.

The Payroll Management System

In 1979, the city's payroll system was revised but retained earlier time-consuming manual methods of preparing output. Payroll clerks continued to convert information from time sheets to wage and salary totals by use of hand calculators and by entering these amounts on forms that were sent to FISA for key punching. Individual cards were used to accumulate a record of the employee's payroll history. Clerical errors and excessive preparation time were major problems.

By 1980, the system's chronic inability to produce paychecks on time produced a crisis in which the principal union formally charged that its members' contractual rights were being violated. The outcome was an agreement by the unions and the mayor's office to form a task force to develop a new system. After some experimentation with alternative arrangements, the present Payroll Management System was designed and was installed in the first agency in early 1984. Five agencies were making use of the system by the end of 1984 with fifteen more adoptions expected by July 1985 and the remainder by mid-1986.

The new system provides for both on-line and paper entry of payroll information to the FISA computer (eventually all agencies will use terminals). Where the paper mode is employed, the operator enters the relevant information in coded form using a specially prepared sheet that can be read by an optical character reader at FISA (employee names are preprinted on entry forms by computer). Where terminals are used, the operator enters the information directly as the names appear in sequence and uses similar codes. Under either arrangement the computer checks for clerical errors and inconsistencies.

The computer not only performs all payroll calculations but keeps a record of overtime, accrues and deaccrues sick leave and annual leave time on the basis of the individual worker's job entitlement, and systematically checks each payroll entry against maximum overtime allowed. Moreover, the system is programmed to recompute all wages *ex post* when new contracts call for wage increases extending retroactively to an earlier official settlement date, and the system maintains a record of past wage and overtime information for each employee. The new system has made it possible for the city to meet promptly its regular payroll obligations and to execute overtime payment and general pay increases in a timely fashion with great reductions in clerical effort. Such payments had in the past been a major source of friction, with delays running into many months, which resulted in general worker dissatisfaction even when pay increases were being awarded.

Not only is payment carried out more promptly, accurately, and with great reduction in clerical effort, but management is provided with information not hitherto available. Although the system is not yet capable of delivering a full range of information to agencies on line, the Office of Payroll Administration (OPA) (which is the principal agent for administration and coordination of the system) provides each user agency on a bi-weekly basis a tape containing all relevant payroll information, thereby permitting the agency to manipulate the data on its microcomputers as desired. All the major agencies use this arrangement, although smaller agencies do not as yet take advantage of this service. In addition, FISA prepares on a regular basis a variety of reports relating to payroll performance.

Introduction of the system has involved significant reorganization. In the words of the executive director of OPA, "It's left the skin of the organizations the same but moved players around." A major reorganizational step was the creation of OPA, which has played a major role in devising and instituting the system, training personnel, and coordinating the system's operation. OPA has assumed important "overhead" functions (functions not specific to the agency) by assuming responsibility for remittance of state and federal taxes withheld from payrolls and for "deductions" such as garnishments, health insurance payments, union dues, IRAs, and death benefits.

Another important organizational change has been the assumption by the Personnel Department of certain functions previously performed at least in part by payroll administrators. The Personnel Department now directly enters the individual into the payroll system after hiring and audits all payrolls of agencies to ensure that individual records are in compliance with various civil service and union requirements.

But the most important changes have occurred within the agencies as a result of new procedures for preparing payroll information and processing and recording information. Not only have procedures for preparing new payrolls been changed, but the new system has made it unnecessary to maintain duplicate records of payroll history within the agency, thereby reducing clerical needs for these tasks. OPA estimates the number of reductions of clerical positions relating to payroll entry alone in three agencies as follows: One agency has eliminated twenty-one positions out of about seventy; a second is in a position to eliminate ten out of twenty-seven, but the exact number remains to be negotiated; and a third that had formerly designated eleven and one-half positions to this work now requires nine, although here, too, the exact number affected remains to be negotiated. Nevertheless, because of standing policy, no one has lost his or her job. Adjustments are made by reassignment and, in time, by attrition.

Training of payroll personnel in the agencies has involved a major effort. During the period prior to instituting the new system workers were given two weeks of formal procedural training spread over a one-month period (one-half of each workday) and carried out away from the job. In addition, where on-line processing was involved each worker was sent to FISA for four to six days of training in use of the terminal (availability and use of the various screens, etc.). OPA also sends skilled personnel to each agency to oversee the new operation for the first three payroll periods of operation. Once the system is instituted in an agency, all new personnel are trained separately by FISA.

The Personnel Reporting and Information System (PRISE)

The administrative office of the Personnel Department contains long rows of file cabinets containing index cards that record the work history of a half million past and present employees of the City of New York. By July 1987, the contents of these cards, traditionally the heart of the city's personnel record system, will have been transcribed into the memory of the department's computer to become a central part of the new personnel reporting and information system (PRISE).

To appreciate the sophistication of this system and the extent of its contribution to administrative efficiency it is necessary to recognize the complex and multiple functions that the Department of Personnel performs. In addition to training and designing and administering qualifying examinations for initial employment and for promotion to virtually all the city's nine hundred-odd job classifications, the department is responsible for certifying all hirings and promotions (determining that individuals being considered for employment or for promotion meet all requirements in terms of test score ranking, seniority, educational or experience history, etc.). It is also responsible for payroll audit (ensuring that payroll information is correct in terms of certain civil service, union contract, and other criteria) and tracking employee history (determining that individuals have proper seniority for promotion, reviewing individual work histories prior to retirement for pension purposes, etc.).

The new system, an on-line management information system, is integrated with the payroll system so that all relevant data and facts on a given employee can be called up not only by personnel, the payroll administration, and the civil service administration, but by the various agencies. Thus far only two agencies can access information from the system using terminals, and all agencies continue to make use of their own personnel record systems for internal records systems. By 1987, all mayoral agencies are expected to have access to the system, and in the years immediately following, nonmayoral agencies will join the system.

The contributions to administrative efficiency to date are impressive. One dramatic example is the department's ability to process the records of a new employee and put him or her on the payroll promptly. Under the old paper-oriented system delays might run into months; under the new system many employees' records can be processed in a few hours, all within a week.[12] A second example is the department's increased ability to respond to new employment needs within the complex framework of civil service requirements. A request from the mayor for, say, 3,000 new police applicants sets the system in motion to produce a list of persons who have passed the appropriate examination, along with rankings of their examination scores and other needed information, including education, experience, sex, and race.

Finally, the system alters personnel administration at the agency level. Not only does it eliminate the duplication of work history records, but it makes personnel information available on line to administrators in a form appropriate for managerial analysis.

As the system is not yet fully implemented, it is not possible to determine how many jobs will be eliminated. Within the Personnel Department sixty employees, on average, since July 1982 have been transferring information from cards to data base. By mid-1987, this work will be completed, and those involved will be free for reassignment. Moreover, there should be an elimination of work in the agencies when duplicate card systems are no longer required. According to one administrator in the Department of Personnel, there should also be a marked reduction in the Bureau of Civil Service Office where old-time methods are being replaced as a result of PRISE. He remarked that the personnel of that bureau might be reduced to "a skeleton crew."

Streetlight Maintenance System

One of the primary responsibilities of the Department of General Service (DGS) is to maintain the city's thousands of streetlights. Complaints regarding nonfunctioning lights are received by DGS staff from the general public and inspection teams; these complaints are transmitted to contractors who perform the maintenance under an agreement whereby failure to repair reported breakdowns within a given period results in a penalty.

Prior to the new computerized system, streetlight maintenance was highly inefficient. Broken lights were so frequently left unrepaired after complaints that the public had in large measure ceased to report them. The system of reporting complaints and monitoring repairs was so unwieldy that it was not feasible for the DGS to deal with more than one contractor for the entire city. Thus the system eliminated from consideration a number of efficient smaller contractors who would have been able to bid on maintenance work only in a more restricted area. When, several years ago, the "winning" contractor submitted an unrealistically low bid and proved unable to deliver promised services, the ensuing crisis led to the design and introduction of the present computerized system as well as to a revision of the bidding and selection process in order to award contracts to smaller firms.

The new system incorporates a geosupport system (see Appendix A) that locates complaints precisely and reports them on line to the responsible contractor. Contractors are required to report back on line when repairs are completed, thereby permitting the system to be monitored continuously. DGS teams certify that contractors are carrying out scheduled work as reported, and the teams also report broken lights.

The city's experience with the new streetlight maintenance system is particularly instructive—it illustrates how operations may be made more efficient when organizations are linked through on-line facilities. A system that had become virtually unworkable under older paper-driven technology became flexible and efficient when a modern computer system utilizing telecommunications networking was put in place.

The DGS experience with the streetlight maintenance system also highlights the importance of organizational change in creating efficient modern computer systems. A senior DGS executive who played a major role in the design and implementation of the system recalled that after the system had been installed for some months, operations proved to be less efficient than had been expected. Although a number of technical problems had been noted, he was convinced that the chief difficulty lay in faulty management. Careful study revealed that a number of managers were continuing to process complaints brought in by inspection teams in the old paper-oriented way rather than allowing the complaints to be entered into the system for automatic transmittal to contractors. It was only after he was able to "get every desk in the place cleaned out" that the system worked efficiently. The managers could then take on new responsibilities rather than process paper.

Computerization in the City Today: An Assessment

In Chapter 1, I pointed out that the way in which work is affected in an organization is closely related to the extent to which new-era

TABLE 2.2
Computer Expenditures per Employee, 1982

Agency/Department	Computer Budget/Employee ($)
Correction	324
Environmental Protection	701
Finance	2,397
Fire	306
General Services (except CSC)	587
HRA	1,800
Health	577
Housing Preservation and Development	1,051
Parks and Recreation	15
Police	348
Sanitation	97
Transportation	1,404

Source: Office of Computer Plans and Controls, unpublished memorandum, June 20, 1983. Data for the New York Housing Authority, Health and Hospitals Corporation, and the Board of Education were not available.

technology has been applied because modern systems bring new work and organizational arrangements. It is not enough to ask whether computers are in use; one must know just how far the process of computerization has progressed. Accordingly, it is important to recognize that New York City, in spite of significant advances since the late 1970s, has moved only part of the way toward adoption of this technology.

None of the city's major systems is designed at present to provide substantial distributed processing capability. Each has on-line capability that provides users with access to a range of information in highly useful form, but none at present allows full-fledged processing at user terminals.[13] Although these sophisticated systems do facilitate major advances in administrative efficiency, changes in organization and work have thus far been less extensive than would be the case where state-of-the-art technology and practice exist. In addition, agencies vary widely in the extent to which they make use of computerization to increase administrative and operational efficiency.

Some evidence of such variation can be found by examining agency computer expenditure budgets, adjusted for differences in levels of employment. Measures for 1982 are presented in Table 2.2 for those mayoral agencies with more than 1,000 employees. Needless to say, the wide variations in the measures reflect to a considerable extent the nature of the agencies' operations and their special requirements for computer assistance. The four agencies with the largest computer budgets per employee have critical needs for computerized systems: the Department of Finance, with its tax assessments and collections; HRA, with its extensive welfare program; the Department of Housing and Development, with its multiple missions, including the management of the city's housing stock and enforcement of the Housing Maintenance Code; and the Department of Transportation, with its broad responsibilities, which range from maintenance of streets and bridges and regulation of traffic to adjudication of parking violations.

But the measures also reflect variations in progressiveness. For example, the two agencies with the lowest adjusted budgets, the Department of Parks and Recreation and the Department of Sanitation, are agencies with widely dispersed operations and large work forces. They would appear to be likely candidates for substantial expenditures on modern management technology. The recent inauguration of the new SCAN network, which computerized the Department of Sanitation scheduling system, confirms the department's earlier need for computerization.

But it is not enough to determine the extent to which the city now utilizes modern technology. It must also be recognized that there are developmental processes at work. The true significance of what is happening as regards the computerization of New York City government is not readily apparent on the surface. A considerable effort is still being allocated to work related to new systems that is purely transitional in nature (e.g., the transposition of the contents of personnel cards to the computer). At the same time, there are new systems and applications that are only partially in place (e.g., PRISE and the Payroll Management System) or are still in process of being developed (e.g., the as-yet-unfinished purchasing system); and there are many partially modernized systems (where new and old technology coexist) and uncomputerized activities that await total conversion to modern practice. All this is unfinished work that promises considerable change in the years immediately ahead.

Moreover, the major sources of change would appear to lie in the area of new applications of computerization. This is particularly true in the case of PCs, which were introduced in recent years. Their use by middle and upper management for tasks ranging from scheduling work to planning agency expenditures, estimating personnel needs, and tracking complex operations is likely to become more and more common. Moreover, such applications as automatic timekeeping (with on-line tie-ins to the payroll system) have as yet only been utilized on an experimental basis.

Computerization and Changes in Work

The thrust of modern computerization is toward the reduction of low-level clerical work and an alteration of the content of clerical and managerial work so that increased attention to managerial control and strategic planning is possible. Moreover, we have seen that modern computer-telecommunications can be applied to a variety of operational tasks within city government such as inspection, engineering design, tracking, vehicle refueling. Does this mean that the occupational composition of the city's work force is being altered, and, if so, is it being altered in such a way as to reduce the relative importance of lower-skilled personnel or to upgrade the skill requirements of part or all of the work force?

A Restructured Work Force?

Some indications of change in the occupational composition of the city's work force can be found in Equal Employment Opportunity Commission (EEOC) employment data for mayoral agencies in 1975 and 1980. Total employment declined from 134,532 to 111,622, but the changes in the various occupational classes were by no means proportional (Table 2.3). The largest changes were employment declines of 8,481, 6,950, and 6,120 in office and clerical workers, protective service (largely police and firefighters), and service workers respectively. Employment increased by 3,454 in the officials and administrators occupational classification. The employment shifts (gains and losses computed after factoring out change that would be expected if employment in each occupational class had declined in the same proportion as overall employment) were greatest in three categories: officials and administrators, an increase of 4,170; office and clerical, a decrease of 3,399; and service workers, a decrease of 2,220.

Clearly, there was a shift of some sort from lower-skilled, lower-paid to higher-skilled, higher-paid employment, but care must be taken not to overestimate the significance of this shift. Changes may reflect, at least in part, the influence of seniority and political pressures during a period of retrenchment when lower-skilled personnel are most vulnerable to layoff. They also may reflect the need for a larger managerial force to cope with the increased pressures for accountability being exerted by state, federal, and watchcare agencies in the wake of the financial crisis. Nevertheless, it is difficult to avoid the conclusion that the increased employment of officials and administrators was affected by the need to implement the major push to computerization that occurred during the

TABLE 2.3
Employment and Employment Change for All NYC Mayoral Agencies, 1975–1980

Job Category	1975 Employment (1)	Employment % (2)	1980 Employment (3)	Employment % (4)	Expected Change[a] (5)	Actual Change (6)	Shift (6)-(5)
Officials and administrators	4,205	3.1	7,659	6.9	−716	+3,454	+4,170
Professionals	21,364	15.9	17,926	16.1	−3,638	−3,438	+200
Technicians	9,801	7.3	8,382	7.5	−1,669	−1,419	+250
Protective service	40,443	30.1	33,493	30.0	−6,887	−6,950	−63
Paraprofessionals	3,172	2.3	2,922	2.6	−540	−250	+290
Office and clerical	29,844	22.2	21,363	19.1	−5,082	−8,481	−3,399
Skilled workers	2,802	2.1	3,096	2.8	−477	+294	+771
Service workers	22,901	17.0	16,781	15.0	−3,900	−6,120	−2,220
Total	134,532	100.0	111,622	100.0	−22,909	−22,910	0

[a] Change that would have occurred if employment in each occupation had changed at the same rate as overall employment.

Source: Equal Employment Opportunity Commission, unpublished data.

latter years of the period and that the declines (both absolute and relative) in office and clerical jobs were to some extent brought about (or at least facilitated) by computerization.

This finding is consistent with the statements of the executives who were interviewed. Each added that workers had been shifted to other duties, a perception that was no doubt correct for individual cases. But the overall result of a declining need for such workers was to make it possible for the city to bring about a reduction in employment through attrition.

Change in Work Content: Clerical Workers and Managerial Personnel

The data in Table 2.3 tell us nothing, however, regarding changes in occupational content. Do the new systems bring about a broadening of responsibility placed on the worker or a demand for mastery of a wider range of procedures?

It is evident that changes in work were sufficiently great to necessitate extensive training at all levels of clerical and managerial work. This was clear in the IFMS experience, and interviews indicated that the experience with other systems has been much the same. But this is by no means proof that the new work is of a higher skill level and requires a better qualified worker. Can we find evidence that sheds light on this issue?

Those workers affected by assignment to word processing and data entry tasks have taken the position that the training and new work procedures involved constitute a higher skill level and have demanded and obtained through their union higher levels of pay. On the other hand, the interview evidence is inconclusive. Most of the managers who had played key roles in bringing on-line systems into being felt that something more was now required of workers involved in the systems and in word processing, that they needed to be a little "smarter." One experienced MIS executive maintained, however, that when he had been shorthanded in terms of data entry personnel, he had encountered no difficulty in training "ordinary clerks" to do the work in a day's time.

Experience in the Sanitation Department proved an interesting case history of how clerical work was changed. In this agency there is a well-established tradition that holds that except for lower-level clerical jobs and upper-level specialist positions, jobs at all three echelons (the fifty-nine district offices, eleven zone headquarters, and city headquarters) are filled by staff who have served earlier as uniformed sanitation workers. This means that the agency is staffed largely by employees with no more than a high school education, many of whom are minority workers. Yet management anticipated no difficulty in shifting these employees to their new duties when the old reporting-scheduling system was converted to a state-of-the-art, on-line computerized system (SCAN). Pilot experience indicated that only a one-week training period is required for the scheduling staff. The explanation offered for the expected ease of transition was that what is required is an understanding of how the system works and what needs to be done. Workers are well qualified in this regard. Moreover, the computer is "friendly," and keyboarding demands are not great because the staff has used typewriters in the past. In fact, it was noted, the job is easier under the new system because the computer "prompts" when errors of entry are made and checks the accuracy of the schedules being prepared before they become operative.

What can be said regarding higher-level clerical and lower-level managerial personnel? One union official expressed concern about the changing work situation faced by a number of higher-level clerks who prior to computerization had carried out complex data assembly, scheduling, and report preparation of the sort described in Chapter 1. She maintained that these workers were being deskilled and in many instances sidelined with reduced responsibilities.

This may well be the case, especially in view of the fact that the new systems do not as yet incorporate distributed processing capability of the sort that would create opportunities for new analytical work at the agency level. Moreover, the limited number of PCs restricts the opportunity for the building of subsystems for agency-oriented statistical analysis and control. Nevertheless, the agencies are being provided with opportunities to work with more information and are being pressured to reorganize work and procedures in order to increase efficiency. In this environment of change there should be an opening up of opportunities for those with long experience and an understanding of how the organization functions.

In general, the interviews did not deal specifically with management, but one management information services manager who had been in charge of bringing into operation a major system did volunteer that whereas clerical personnel had encountered few problems with training, managers often experienced difficulty in mastering their changed roles. He suggested that the new work for clerks was well defined but the responsibilities for management were not. It seems likely that here, as in the case of some senior clerical people, these systems may have taken away more responsibility than they introduced. It is interesting to note, however, that in the Department of Finance, where there has been an aggressive effort to set up internal systems that utilize PCs to track tax evaders for a number of the city's excise and license taxes, there has been a corresponding creation of new responsibilities for both managerial and seasoned clerical personnel.

On balance, the evidence regarding clerical and managerial work is sketchy and inconclusive. The new clerical work is somewhat more demanding in terms of the degree of responsibility the worker initially assumes and the wider range of procedures that must be mastered. Managerial and some higher-level clerical work will become more sophisticated as more advanced applications of the new technology are introduced. But whether or not city government must raise its hiring requirements in order to secure the caliber of workers it requires is still an unanswered question.

Changes in Work Content: Nonadministrative Personnel

Although the interviews focused on clerical and managerial work, it became clear early in the investigation that computerization has directly or indirectly affected other work as well, including that of inspectors, engineers, police, firefighters, sanitation workers, and even workers dispensing fuel to the city's fleet of vehicles. On the other hand, there are literally thousands of workers whose daily tasks have not as yet been significantly touched by computerization. It seems inherent in the technology that applications will be extended in the years ahead to permit various personnel to receive instructions and to report on inspections and other work. Most MIS executives predicted that in the future virtually everyone will have some contact with the computer system through terminals, cellular modular devices, or handheld computers. It is likely, however, that such changes will come gradually and will not significantly alter the work content of most nonadministrative personnel.

Implications of Computerization for Job Entry and Career Development

Thierry Noyelle found evidence (based on his studies of retailing, banking, and insurance) that introducing modern computer systems raises entry requirements for work and that an interruption of pathways for advancement occurs (a "delinking" of mobility paths) that discriminates against lower-level workers.[14] The latter is considered the result of new demands for educational requirements at managerial and professional levels. It is also the result of supply-side pressures occasioned by a much larger population of college-trained young people who can only be recruited by offering career "tracks" that bring the young employee into the organization at a junior executive or professional level. What is the likelihood that computerization will bring about an upgrading of requirements for job entry and a reduction of career opportunities in the years immediately ahead?

Thus far there have been very significant changes in administrative work that have brought some upgrading of certain lower-level clerical job requirements, but such upgrading does not appear to have extended as yet to nonclerical or to managerial personnel. The major exception to this finding not discussed previously is in the area of skilled computer specialists, where the city has recruited widely from the outside. What is most impressive about this experience, however, is that these new systems have been put into place using the existing work force. In short, a work force already in place, which was recruited by utilizing long-established entry requirements, has proven, albeit with considerable training, capable of meeting the new work demands that have arisen thus far.

In the final analysis what happens in terms of job entry and career opportunities depends on the extent to which the city finds it necessary to recruit from the private sector or from colleges and other training institutions rather than continue making use of its present arrangements for bringing in new workers, training them, and offering them opportunities for advancement. We must consider, then, just how city government functions as an employment system and what role its training arrangements play in facilitating upward mobility.

City government as an employment system. The principal characteristics of the city as an employer can be grouped under two headings: low-entry requirements and arrangements for promotion and occupational change as overseen by the civil service and the unions.

1. City government has traditionally been characterized by low-entry requirements. Examinations must be taken for other than short-term provisional jobs (except for certain professional categories and upper level political appointments), but for lower-level entry work these examinations are quite simple and do not necessarily require a high school degree. The result has been that city government is the largest minority employer and has during the years opened up a host of opportunities for permanent work to men and women who would have otherwise found, at best, only peripheral employment.

2. City government is essentially a huge internal labor market that provides a considerable arena for promotion and occupational change. At the lowest levels all permanent-status entry jobs have formal promotional ladders to a second level of expertise and remuneration and, in principle at least, to a third supervisory level. Qualification for promotion is achieved through experience or educational achievement (in most instances the former can be substituted at least in part for the latter) and by passing examinations. Occupational change within the

overall city system can be effected through examinations and through the necessary experience and/or educational attainment. The system is regulated by well-defined state civil service requirements as well as by provisions that often reflect union bargaining and pressure.

In practice, the system is often cumbersome and inflexible. It is frequently a hindrance to management in improving efficiency and to some employees with initiative and ability who might otherwise move up more quickly. But at the same time, it offers opportunities to large numbers of workers to enter at low levels and move up the occupational hierarchy or to find new careers. For many the opportunities for upward advancement are limited, but for those who have ability and are willing to acquire additional training or additional formal academic credentials, the pathways to upward mobility are well defined and available.

Training within city government. Fundamental to the functioning of the system are the city's extensive training arrangements. Training is carried out in all the major agencies. Many of the courses offered are job specific and allow the worker to acquire needed knowledge for advancement or occupational change. In addition, the principal union (DC 37) also conducts a training institution that emphasizes basic skills such as literacy and elementary mathematics and provides some clerical training. (It is currently planning to offer a course in word processing.)

Changing occupational composition. The employment data presented in Table 2.1 demonstrate not only a decline in overall employment, probably due to the retrenchment efforts of the period, but also a change in occupational composition away from clerical and service worker employment. As these occupational groups are the two major avenues of job entry for workers with limited education and experience, the trend is unfavorable in terms of jobs available to minorities and other groups among the city's poor. Moreover, a continuation of these trends is likely to bring new pressures on administrators to raise hiring requirements at the lower-entry levels and to recruit more actively from universities and specialized training institutions.

The Outlook for Job Entry and Mobility

The New York City government is an enormously complex organization that is deeply involved in the process of adopting new technology, a process that has already brought major changes in work and that promises to bring even more changes in the years just ahead. Thus far the new work requirements have been met for the most part by extensive retraining of the existing work force. There is evidence, however, that some work has become more demanding, although it is not yet apparent that these new demands cannot be met within the city's existing hiring arrangements and standards.

As city government continues to modernize, the patterns of work outlined in Chapter 1 are likely to become more pronounced and to result in an upgrading of occupational content and a change in the occupational matrix toward a decline in the number of lower-level clerical jobs. One possible outcome of this new pattern is that entry requirements at the bottom of the job hierarchy will be raised; another is that recruitment will increasingly take place at the college and university level. Both pose major problems for the City's poor.

The danger is that the internal labor market structure of city government, which has been so effective in the past in bringing opportunities for those least well equipped to find acceptable employment opportunities, will play a less effective role in the years ahead. The policy implications of these dynamics are of three general sorts. First, every effort must be made to strengthen the government's training machinery in order to make it possible to resist pressures to raise entry level requirements. Second, the city's public education and training institutions must be strengthened in order to equip minorities and low-income young people with the basic literacy and computational skills necessary to allow them to compete in a world of work in which use of this technology is pervasive. Third, the applications of the technology will free up resources that can be redirected to new city services that require a different allocation of work effort. The new systems are so powerful that they promise a reduction in the need to allocate human and financial resources for purely administrative tasks. Yet the needs of an urban society for services grows apace. Such economies make it possible for the city to divert resources to provide new or expanded services such as parks, nurseries, cleaner streets, and transport. Here are job opportunities that remain to be exploited.

Notes

1. Interview, March 27, 1984.

2. The Human Resources Administration, whose integrated on-line data processing system dates back to 1972, is the principal exception to this statement.

3. Although the city's history of computerization encompasses three decades and by the mid–1970s had progressed to the point that twelve mayoral agencies were operating computer installations, the Shinn Commission (Mayor Abe Beame's Management Advisory Board), appointed in 1976, concluded after careful investigation that there was a need for an immediate reorganization. The city was spending more than $60 million annually on computers and data processing, but there was no single agency planning or coordinating the system. The

commission recommended the creation of an oversight agency for computer planning, the opening of city-owned data processing centers, and the relaxation of civil service rules so that the city could compete with the private sector in hiring computer specialists. See Desmond Smith, "Brave New City," *New York*, May 14, 1984, p. 60.

4. The others are Police, Fire, Human Resources Administration, Finance, and Housing Preservation and Development.

5. Smith, "Brave New City."

6. Interviews were conducted in the Mayor's Office of Operations, Labor Management Committee Program, Office of Computer Plans and Controls, Computer Service Center, Human Resources Administration, Finance Department, Police Department, Sanitation Department, Health and Hospitals Corporation, Department of General Services, Department of Personnel, Office of Payroll Administration, and District Council 37 American Federation of State, County and Municipal Employees, AFL-CIO.

7. It is interesting that financial justification may come by any of several routes. In some instances (e.g., tracking tax noncompliance and parking violations) it may bring in additional revenues; in others it may reduce labor costs; and in still others it may simply be less expensive than older technologies in nonlabor terms (eliminating more expensive teletype arrangements, reducing bids from suppliers by closer control, improving purchasing, eliminating waste, and reducing inventories).

8. This estimate is the author's, based on information contained in a survey of forty-five mayoral agencies by District Council 37 in late 1984.

9. *The Mayor's Management Report*, September 17, 1984, NYCPB section, p. 3.

10. This discussion follows closely, with quotations, material presented in The Urban Academy, *An Introduction to IFMS*, 2nd ed. (New York, December 1977), pp. 1-11.

11. Ibid., p. 125.

12. These estimates do not include the interval necessary for sending fingerprints of some new employees to Albany for checking. Here the delay may still involve several weeks.

13. These major systems include, in addition to the four discussed above, the new Department of Sanitation scheduling system, the Departments of Police and Fire dispatching systems, the Department of General Services streetlight maintenance system, and the HRA welfare management system.

14. Thierry Noyelle, *Beyond Industrial Dualism: Market and Job Segmentation in the New Economy* (Boulder, Colo.: Westview, 1987).

3

Computerization in Hospitals

U.S. hospitals today face two crises. On the one hand, they are increasingly being pressured to reduce costs in response to new forms of competition and methods of remuneration; on the other hand, they are being forced to redefine their roles as deliverers of health services. Computer-telecommunications technology offers opportunities to reduce costs and improve efficiency. Yet at the same time, this technology confronts management with critical problems of adaptation and requires substantial capital expenditures.

The objectives of this chapter are to examine the recent experience of hospitals in computerizing their operations, to assess the pace at which these systems and their applications are being installed, and to analyze the impact of adaptation on work and career opportunities. The study is based largely upon interviews with executives of seven hospitals and the Hospital Corporation of America (HCA) as well as with a number of individuals closely associated with the industry. Material also was drawn from articles in the major hospital management journals and from publications of the Empire Medical Plan of New York (formerly Blue Cross–Blue Shield of Greater New York) and Health Research and Educational Trust of New Jersey. Case studies of one hospital, New Hanover Memorial Hospital, Wilmington, North Carolina, and HCA are presented in Appendix B.

The New Environment

The crisis facing U.S. hospitals today can only be understood by recognizing the decades of growth and rising medical costs that preceded the recent years of mounting difficulties. Under conditions of rising demand for health care and permissive practices in which public sector and third-party payer reimbursement was made on the basis of the costs submitted by individual hospitals, employment grew rapidly (from 1.6 million full-time employees in 1960 to 3.7 million in 1981); the rises in the costs of medical services in hospitals far exceeded the increases in the costs of living (for example, the price index of hospital room charges rose by 964 percent from 1960 to 1983 compared to an increase in the consumer price index of 235 percent).[1] This era of affluence and loose control set the stage for major difficulties when the 1980s brought declining demand and new constraints on public and private sector payers.

Declining demand was at first largely incipient for most hospitals (there was a decline in hospital inpatient days per 1,000 population in every year but one after 1965), but since 1981 there has been a continuous decline in inpatient census.[2] This decline has been due to a number of causes, including technological changes, efforts by both public and private sector payers to reduce the costs of medical services, and new sources of competition arising out of institutional changes and modes of practice.

Payment for both Medicare and Medicaid patients in hospitals has been significantly changed since 1981 when requirements for Medicaid were altered to permit states to reduce reimbursement. But the most dramatic change occurred in 1983 with the introduction of the prospective payment system, which replaced older arrangements by which hospitals were paid on the basis of historical costs. Under prospective payment, hospitals are reimbursed for the treatment of Medicare patients on the basis of a fixed amount per case, depending on the diagnosis as classified in a list of 467 diagnosis-related groups (DRGs), regardless of the actual costs of treatment.

At the same time, private sector employers have increasingly pressured Blue Cross and other third-party payers to reduce or at least contain the costs of providing health insurance for their employees and have sought alternative arrangements for the provision of medical care. Some indication of the strength of this new development is seen in the increased number of insurance plans requiring a front-end deductible for inpatient charges, from 30 percent in 1982 to 63 percent in 1984, and in a sharp increase in the number of firms insisting on some sort of utilization review of patient management or second surgical opinion.[3]

Medical technology has made major advances in recent years, which have resulted in more effective treatment, a reduction in the number of days of hospitalization, and less-invasive surgery. For example, the number of surgical procedures handled on an ambulatory basis rose from a level estimated as ranging from 6 to 10 percent of all such procedures in 1970 to approximately 20 percent in 1983.[4]

Among the major changes in medical practice and institutional arrangements have been the increasing use of physicians' offices as sites for procedures and tests previously performed within the hospital and new or at least rapidly growing alternative institutional arrangements, including health maintenance organizations (HMOs), voluntary hospital organizations, preferred provider organizations (PPOs), ambulatory surgical centers (ASCs), and for-profit hospitals.[5]

It is within this sharply altered environment that all hospitals, both nonprofit and for-profit, must seek patients. Not only is there growing pressure for cost reduction, but there is growing competition among a larger group of service organizations. Thus, we see that hospitals face new and difficult challenges, challenges that create an increased need for modern computer systems.

Why Hospitals Need Computers: Complexity of Production and Administration

Although hospitals vary widely in terms of size, range and types of treatment, and basic organizational form (i.e., nonprofit, governmental, or private), all are candidates for computerization across a broad spectrum of activities. To understand why, it must be recognized that hospitals are highly complex organizations and for a number of reasons are difficult to manage and that computer-telecommunications technology is widely applicable within these complex organizations. The complexity of the modern hospital arises out of the nature of its products, the multiplicity of its inputs and lack of standardization in modes of treatment, the complex arrangements by which it is remunerated, the highly detailed reporting and recordkeeping requirements to which it must comply, and the diffused management and lack of centralized top-down control that for both historical and institutional reasons have come to characterize its operation. This section addresses the sources of complexity and problems of management; the following section, the broad applicability of computer systems within the hospital.

Multiple Products

Essentially, the hospital is a large job order shop specializing in the production of a wide range of unstandardized "products"—treatment of a large number of patients with widely varying disabilities. Just how many different treatments a given hospital will administer in the course of a year is difficult to estimate. The number, even for a small, general care hospital, is likely to be very large indeed. Patients vary not only in terms of their basic illnesses and conditions but also in severity of illness, age and general state of health, and presence of complications. Each such variation in the condition of the patient is likely to make necessary a variation in the treatment itself.

An additional complication for the large teaching hospital is that the mission of the institution is not restricted to patient care. Two other responsibilities must be carried out by the staff: the pursuit of research and instruction of students, residents, nurse trainees, and other specialized personnel.

Multiple Inputs

If the hospital is defined as a job order shop, then it also must be defined as one with a wide range of inputs. Each hospital is organized around a number of departments specializing in the production of intermediate products that are inputs to the total patient care process or in the provision of basic housekeeping, administrative, or managerial support. But the analogy is complicated by a fundamental difference: The production protocol for a given patient's treatment is established not by a central manager (and, accordingly, fixed for a considerable period of time) but by staff doctors who are likely to differ in the combination of inputs prescribed (e.g., medication, diet, nursing care, laboratory and radiology procedures, and length of stay). The net result is that provision of inputs even for roughly similar treatment is likely to be unstandardized.

Complex Billing, Accounting, and Reporting

Not unexpectedly, the wide variety of conditions treated and the multiplicity of procedures and medications prescribed result in complex billing and accounting. The accounting system must bring together a host of direct and indirect costs, and under the new prospective payment requirements these costs must be assigned on a patient-by-patient basis.[6] To add to the complexity, the hospital receives revenues from a number of sources. Third-party payers (Blue Cross–Blue Shield, Medicare, Medicaid, various major medical insurers, and corporate benefits systems) must be billed separately and according to different arrangements, as must patients as residual payers, and collections from each must be made. In addition, the hospital receives a variety of grants and donations, each of which is likely to be earmarked for specific types of expenditures. All of these must be administered within the accounting system.

Moreover, the demands upon the hospital staff for reports and record maintenance are heavy indeed. Not only do third-party payers demand extensive reports and the opportunity to review costs, but state and medical groups also may require reports. Records and reports necessary for the day-to-day administration of patient care constitute an even greater burden. Doctors' and nurses' notes, records of all orders, procedures executed and medication administered, final abstracts by the physician in charge and the surgeon (where applicable) must be filed in the patient's record and maintained by the Medical Records Department.[7] The author was advised by a leading surgeon that a single patient's file might easily contain fifty pieces of paper—a total annual accumulation of medical records in a 400-bed hospital of close to 1 million pieces of paper! In addition, departments such as clinical laboratory, radiology, pharmacy, and physical therapy must maintain patient records, and all departments, whether directly involved with patient care or not, must maintain administrative records to ensure proper functioning.

Complex Problems of Management

Perhaps the most unique characteristic of the hospital as a production center is that the production process is managed not by a single managerial organization at the top but by physicians. Orders as well as patient supervision must come from the doctor in charge. Accordingly, complex health care delivery processes are planned and monitored not by a production manager answerable to top management but by a number of individual managers, each of whom is intermittently giving instructions and requiring information on the patient's condition.

Hospitals also face complex problems in the management of their human resources. Total labor costs are high; even the smallest hospital employs a variety of professionals and technically specialized personnel in addition to clerical workers, service and maintenance workers, and stockkeepers. Moreover, the hospitals must be staffed around the clock, and many employees work irregular and part-time schedules (e.g., nurses are increasingly employed part-time to permit adjustment to varying patient loads).

The Legacy of the Past: Creaky Paper-Ridden Operations and Uncontrolled Costs

Implicit in the preceding descriptions is that hospitals are difficult to manage. The old-time hospital unassisted by technology was at best a creaky paper-ridden operation. Each patient's admission set in motion a lengthy, complex process of ordering, scheduling, recordkeeping, and reporting, while a fragmented, decentralized organizational structure necessitated multiple—and frequently duplicative—paper systems for recordkeeping and management. This elaborate paper-oriented mode of operation is a legacy of the past that today's hospital management must somehow modernize through technology and improved management.

But there is yet another set of problems facing hospitals today: the legacy of past tendencies toward high-cost operations brought on by years of operation under retrospective cost criteria for third-party payment. Until recently, hospitals simply billed third-party payers—Blue Cross–Blue Shield, major medical insurers, Medicare and Medicaid administrators—on the basis of estimated historical costs. To be sure, as the costs of medical care mounted, third-party payers demanded some kind of accounting, but always on the basis of historical records and with no effective arrangement for assuring that medical services were rendered efficiently.

Problems Facing Management Today

As a result of this combination of inherently complex production arrangements, lack of effective management at the top, and poorly developed cost controls, hospital management today is faced with a daunting array of problems that include: (1) eliminating excessive treatment costs, especially those arising from unnecessary ordering procedures and medication and/or involving excessive lengths of stay; (2) scheduling patient treatment and maintaining effective communication among all the parties responsible for patient care in order to prevent delays and human errors; (3) controlling purchases and inventories of the vast array of pharmaceuticals, supplies, and equipment to reduce costs while assuring that stockouts and breakdowns do not occur; (4) conforming the system of cost control, case review, and reporting to the new requirements of prospective payment practice; (5) coping with an ever growing burden of recordkeeping, reporting, and complex billing and collections; and (6) managing personnel to maximize utilization of human potential, improve morale, and increase efficiency.

For the most part hospitals are ill prepared to cope with these problems. The retrospective payment arrangements of the past required little attention to departmental efficiency and none to monitoring treatment of individual patients to eliminate unneeded or unnecessary procedures and medication. Cost and clinical information were related only casually and crudely, if at all, and little effort was made to reduce the heavy burden of clerical work performed throughout the organization or to speed up communication throughout the service centers that made up the total organization. Now hospitals must convert to new and quite different arrangements dictated by the requirements of prospective payment and do so within a brief span of time. They require new information and organizational arrangements to meet this challenge. Old-time paper systems or even old-era computer systems are inadequate. Meeting the challenge to convert to DRG-compatible operations requires application of computer-telecommunications technology.

Hospital Computerization:
Range of Applications and Types of Systems

It is apparent from the discussion of computerization in Chapter 1 that the new-era technology should be widely applicable to the problems facing hospital management today. Although it is impossible to describe here the conceivable applications of computer-telecommunications technology, some sense of the range of possible applications can be gained by examining Figure 3.1 and Table 3.1. Figure 3.1, reproduced from the Blue Cross–Blue Shield of Greater New York hospital vendor survey,[8] presents seven "component" areas of a total hospital computerization and under each component lists from six to ten categories of application—a total of fifty-two in all. In the Blue Cross–Blue Shield volume this table served as a guide to sixty-nine pages of tabular presentation in which specific computerized functions were listed—a total of more than 1,200 computerized functions.[9] Table 3.1 is a sample of this latter material and lists the functions of one component, clinical laboratory management.

Although the material in Figure 3.1 and Table 3.1 is sketchy, even a quick reading indicates that virtually every aspect of hospital operations—from preadmission and nursing station to housekeeping and strategic planning—can be supported by computerization.

The Blue Cross–Blue Shield vendor survey presented information on the systems offered by four major vendors. Each vendor offered two or more large systems with a number of applications that were available either as a complete system or as separate modules. If the entire field of vendors had been canvassed, it would have been apparent that an extremely wide assortment of large and small systems, stand-alone applications, and special software applications were available in the marketplace. Moreover, a review of products introduced in the years since publication of the survey would reveal a rapid proliferation of new systems and a host of special applications.

Types of Computer Systems

As there will be frequent reference to a number of computer systems in the subsequent sections, a brief description of the nature and purpose of the principal types is included here. These statements may be read in conjunction with the list of applications in Figure 3.1.

Financial and administrative systems (financial support, administrative support, general services/miscellaneous). These systems include inpatient and outpatient billing, accounts receivable, accounts payable, payroll and personnel, purchasing, and general ledger applications. Older systems are likely to operate only in the batch processing mode; newer systems

FIGURE 3.1
Major Components of a Modern Comprehensive Hospital Computer System, with Categories of Applications

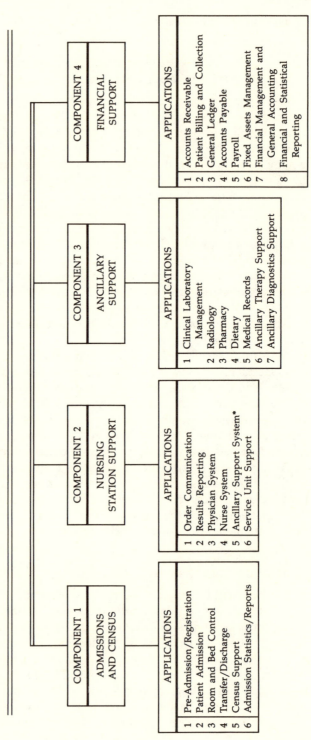

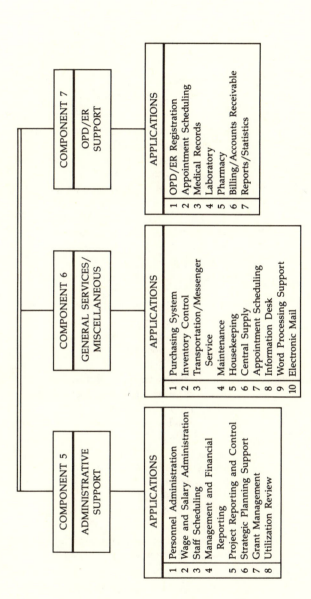

COMPONENT 5	COMPONENT 6	COMPONENT 7
ADMINISTRATIVE SUPPORT	GENERAL SERVICES/ MISCELLANEOUS	OPD/ER SUPPORT

APPLICATIONS

1 Personnel Administration
2 Wage and Salary Administration
3 Staff Scheduling
4 Management and Financial Reporting
5 Project Reporting and Control
6 Strategic Planning Support
7 Grant Management
8 Utilization Review

APPLICATIONS

1 Purchasing System
2 Inventory Control
3 Transportation/Messenger Service
4 Maintenance
5 Housekeeping
6 Central Supply
7 Appointment Scheduling
8 Information Desk
9 Word Processing Support
10 Electronic Mail

APPLICATIONS

1 OPD/ER Registration
2 Appointment Scheduling
3 Medical Records
4 Laboratory
5 Pharmacy
6 Billing/Accounts Receivable
7 Reports/Statistics

*Applications are performed by interface with systems located elsewhere. For example, OPD/ER support systems are interfaced with laboratory and pharmacy systems to obtain information and submit orders.

Source: Blue Cross–Blue Shield of Greater New York, *Hospital Information System Vendor Survey,* Vol. 1, 1982-1983 (New York, N.Y.: Blue Cross–Blue Shield of Greater New York, 1983), p. 36. Reprinted by permission.

52

TABLE 3.1
Example of Range of Computerized Functions Available in a Modern Comprehensive Computer System: Clinical Laboratory Management

Function	Applications
Order entry	On-line service requests and entry from multiple terminal locations Automatic entry of order in patient data base Automatic worksheet generation
Status inquiry	Retrieval and merger of archival results by patient ID, clinic, physician Automatic alert for drug interaction with requested test Cumulative preadmission lab summaries
Results reporting	Ability to verify results before reporting CRT result reporting by patient Direct result capture from dedicated laboratory instruments
Laboratory inventory management	Cost allocation-supplies and equipment Ability to enter manual results on pre-formatted screens Specimen label printing
Automatic interface	Census (ADT) Financial applications Medical records
Laboratory management reports	Daily workloads (by test, lab section, ordering unit) Monthly and annual workload levels Cost/test calculations

Source: Blue Cross–Blue Shield of Greater New York, *Hospital Information System Vendor Survey*, Vol. 1, 1982-1983 (New York, N.Y.: Blue Cross–Blue Shield, 1983).

offer on-line, real-time applications. In recent years budgeting and decision support applications have become available.

Admissions-discharge transfer (ADT) systems (admissions and census). ADT systems assist the Admissions Department in registering patients, keeping records of patient visits (although not the patients' clinical records), and informing nursing stations and ancillary departments of the patient's location. Basic functions supported include assisting the Admissions Department by preparing various admitting documents without retyping basic information and by expediting the processing of new patients; providing various census reports on a routine and/or inquiry basis; and keeping track of each patient's room and bed. A computerized ADT system is an essential component of an on-line hospital information system (see below). When linked to ancillary departments the ADT system provides the patient's name and number, which can be utilized for automatic labeling of forms, reports, prescriptions, and so on. One of the most useful functions of such automated systems is to eliminate the retyping of basic patient information throughout the hospital.

Nursing systems (nursing station support). Nursing systems provide for electronic communication of doctors' orders and nurses station requisitions to ancillary departments and may provide communication of test results, procedures carried out, and prescriptions filled.[10] The simplest systems provide only entry of orders and collection of charges and are called data collection or order entry systems. The more complex systems, known as Hospital Information Systems (HIS), retrieve results and usually perform a variety of other functions that might include nurse care planning and nurses station medication control. HIS also may provide the physician with access for ordering or retrieving results through terminals in the doctors' lounge, in other points in the hospital, or even in the individual doctor's office.

Ancillary departments (ancillary support). These systems (including pharmacy, radiology, clinical laboratory) may be relatively simple or quite sophisticated. The most modern systems will record and print out results and may be linked to HIS systems for reporting. Systems also may provide technical information useful to the professional or technician as well as a file of results of past tests and procedures and administrative support such as inventory control information.

Outpatient Department and Emergency Room support (OPD/ER support). These systems provide basic registration and scheduling support. Where HIS systems are in operation, OPD/ER systems will be linked to the main system to provide access to a variety of patient-related information (Figure 3.1).

New-Era Versus Old-Era Technology

In Chapter 1, I distinguished between old- and new-era technology and noted that the earlier period of application was largely confined to "number-crunching," with data processed in the batch mode by hardware located in the computer center and with little or no use of telecommunications. New-era technology is bringing more powerful hardware, greatly expanded memory, and greater use of on-line systems. Thus, various parts of the organization can be networked so that computing can be distributed outward to departments and branch operations and data bases of both financial and clinical information can be built, drawn upon, or added to anywhere within the organization. This technology is not, however, limited to on-line data-base systems; it allows the user to employ versatile and relatively inexpensive micro- and minicomputers in the stand-alone mode for specialized applications or to link with the larger computer as part of an integrated system.

Hospitals thus face a wide range of options in making use of the new technology. Large distributed systems can maximize computing capability and interdepartmental linkages, but smaller subsystems and stand-alone installations can also be extremely valuable for a host of applications such as laboratory, pharmacy, and radiology operations, DRG analysis, and scheduling of personnel and patients. Of special importance is the opportunity offered by the extended menu of available hardware and software to computerize incrementally by installing the new technology as need and financial capability dictate and combining the pieces in time to build larger and more powerful systems.

Variations in Experience and Changing Strategies

Some Evidence of Unevenness

Most hospitals have long made use of computers in some operations; yet the extent to which computerization has been brought to bear on various activities within the hospital has varied widely. The data presented in Table 3.2 provide evidence of this unevenness of computerization, but they probably understate the extent of variation because the data do not indicate the level of sophistication and range of functions implied when a given hospital reports an application as "installed."

The variations in extent of computerization are due to a number of factors, including the cost and cost effectiveness of systems, ease of utilization, and perception of need. For example, the popularity of patient billing/accounts receivable and general ledger is readily explained. Such systems differ little from financial systems used by business and gov-

TABLE 3.2
Percentage of Hospitals with Selected Applications Installed, 1981 and 1984

Selected Applications	1981	1984
Financial management systems		
Patient billing/accounts receivable	92.8	100.0
General ledger	89.2	98.8
Inventory	46.4	57.1
Patient care systems		
Admissions	51.1	78.5
Order entry	13.0	40.4
Medical records	28.5	59.5
Strategic management systems		
Financial planning	35.7	48.8
DRG analysis	0	65.4

Source: Hospitals, January 16, 1985, p. 117.

ernment and have been available in one form or another since the beginning of commercial computerization. They are relatively problem free, are widely recognized to be effective in reducing costs and simplifying administration, and can be operated in the batch mode on relatively unsophisticated equipment or integrated with large modern on-line systems.

On the other hand, the relatively low percentages of hospitals with inventory and order entry systems are due, at least in part, to the fact that these systems tend to be utilized in hospitals where management is relatively progressive and where financial arrangements are relatively unstressed.[11] Order entry systems, in particular, are complex on-line systems requiring considerable capital outlay as well as major planning and adaptation. Computerized inventory management has been slow to win popularity, apparently in large part because of the need to use fairly sophisticated systems to control the variety of items that are held in stock by a number of departments and that are drawn upon unpredictably and in piece-meal fashion.

However, increases in applications from 1981 to 1984 (Table 3.2) are probably of greater interest than are the differences in levels of adoption. The greatest increases were clearly in DRG analysis, medical records, and order entry. All three systems are closely associated with prospective payment and attest to a new focus in computerization. DRG analysis

TABLE 3.3
Percentages of Hospitals with Computer-assisted Medical Records, by Size, 1983

Number of Beds	Percentages
Less than 100	38.7
100–199	48.3
200–299	68.9
300–399	81.3
400–499	84.0
500 and more	87.2
All sizes combined	66.8

Source: Michael Nathanson, "Hospitals Pump Dollars into Finance, Nursing," Modern Healthcare, September 1984, pp. 114–123.

and medical records systems are utilized in the processing and reporting of case information; order entry systems may be used to capture procedures and charges and, where interfaced with financial systems, to transmit this information electronically for billing.

But unevenness in adoption of computerization is not restricted to differences among types of systems. Of at least equal interest are the differences among hospitals in the aggressiveness of effort and level of sophistication of the systems they adopt. Although experience varies, as a group, medium and large hospitals have been in the best position to apply the new technology; small hospitals, the worst. Moreover, when adoption takes place larger hospitals are more likely to install more complex systems. The results of a study of medical records automation in 1983 by Sheldon I. Dorenfest (Table 3.3), discussed in an article by Michael Nathanson, illustrate how computerization may vary among hospitals.[12]

Dorenfest also found that by the end of 1984 about one-fourth of the estimated 5,800 community hospitals were expected to have nursing systems that were at least partly automated, with smaller hospitals making use of systems with limited functions and larger institutions, with more sophisticated systems.[13] Similarly he estimated that 800 hospitals were not equipped with automated billing systems in 1984, and that all of these hospitals were small (fewer than one hundred beds).[14]

Changing Strategies

Because prospective payment has brought about a new emphasis on cost control, such control may be pursued in one of two ways that are by no means mutually exclusive. The first approach is to increase departmental efficiency and thus ensure that laboratory, pharmacy, operating room, dietary facilities, and so on are functioning without waste of personnel or materials. The second approach is to reduce patient stays and to eliminate unnecessary procedures and medications.

A hospital can focus principally on one approach and give little attention to the other. In particular, it is possible for management to emphasize reduction in lengths of stay and examination of physician treatment with an eye to reducing unnecessary procedures and medication. But a thorough campaign to reduce costs must involve both approaches. Ancillary departments must carry out their operations efficiently, and physicians must be induced to eliminate wasteful procedures and to avoid hospitalizing patients for unnecessarily long periods.

The interviews and the literature emphasized that hospitals simply cannot operate successfully under prospective payment arrangements without the support of computer systems. In the first strategy, computer systems are needed to eliminate paperwork, control inventories, reduce the time required to prepare reports, perform laboratory procedures and x-rays, fill prescriptions, schedule patients, and abridge work in other operational tasks. At the same time, computer systems provide management with the information necessary to supervise and plan operations more effectively.

But these systems are also necessary to pursue the second strategy because only the new technology can provide efficiently and on short notice the information (including detailed costs) on procedures and medications utilized in each patient's care so that treatment can be monitored with an eye to reducing patient stays, economizing the use of resources, and making it possible for management to control and plan for operations.

Accordingly, hospitals have a need for systems that merge financial and medical information, that assist in preparing abstracts for discharge, that facilitate DRG-compatible billing, and that analyze "case-mix" history (making it possible to ask "what if" questions regarding the effect of alternative patterns of patient demand on hospital revenues and costs). But it is also important for hospitals to develop information that will permit cost control. Ideally this requires a cost accounting system that assigns a standard (efficient practice) cost to each procedure; systems that permit concurrent review of treatment and length of stay while the patient is hospitalized; and access to information on past treatment of each given condition within the hospital and, perhaps for comparison, within other hospitals as well.

Development and use of standard costs is a time-honored business procedure but a major innovation among hospitals. In hospitals standard costs must be developed for each procedure in order to establish a basis for DRG reporting, identify costly procedures, and provide a yardstick for cost control through variance analysis within ancillary departments.[15] Concurrent review is an essential part of a process by which hospitals are beginning to move toward a greater standardization of treatment. Under retrospective payment it was difficult for hospital management to hold doctors accountable for wasteful methods of treatment.[16] Under the new arrangements doctors are confronted with the costs of procedures and are taking joint action to reduce unnecessary procedures and excessive stays. Access to information on past treatment is essential in the move toward setting realistic standards. Standardization puts a premium on long-term storage of detailed patient records and brings new emphasis on the need for increased storage capacity.

Computerization in Selected Hospitals: The Interviews

The analysis presented in the remaining sections of this chapter is based upon interviews with executives of seven hospitals and one major private sector multimember hospital organization, the Hospital Corporation of America (HCA). Brief descriptions of each of these organizations is presented below, providing only the special aspects of each organization that are particularly significant to the overall analysis. Case histories of one hospital, New Hanover Memorial, and of HCA are presented in Appendix B. Short case histories of the remaining hospitals will be supplied by the author upon request.[17]

The Institutions Interviewed

New Hanover Memorial Hospital (Wilmington, N.C.), a 526-bed general nonprofit hospital, is representative of a large number of institutions that are using conventional computer technology but are on the brink of introducing many new applications. New Hanover Memorial's present computerized system consists of ADT, accounting, general ledger, payroll, and billing. PCs are used for DRG reporting and in several departments. Inventory and accounts payable are paper systems. An HIS data-base system with functions for administration, order entry, and inventory control is planned.

University Hospital (Stony Brook, N.Y.) is a 540-bed teaching hospital with a totally integrated data-base system in which virtually every phase of the hospital operation is affected by computerization. However, University Hospital's present system does not fully computerize all functions. Nursing and medical records processing and analysis are paper driven.

Beth Israel (Boston, Mass.) is a 452-bed teaching hospital of the Harvard Medical School. Beth Israel's clinical and financial/administrative systems are interfaced, and its clinical system is one of the country's most comprehensive. The hospital has plans for advanced computerization of medical records and DRG analysis.

Columbia Presbyterian Medical Center (New York, N.Y.), a 1,199-bed hospital, is an example of a major hospital that has not made extensive use of modern computer technology but plans a state-of-the-art integrated data-base system in the next few years. Its financial and billing operations are supported by batch-mode computer systems.

New York University Hospital (New York, N.Y.), with 878 beds, has a sophisticated nursing support system that although effective in day-to-day operation offers only limited archival capabilities. Its administrative system is only partly automated, and the hospital's plans for future computerization do not indicate that the hospital will be fully equipped with new-era systems in the near future.

New England Medical Center (Boston, Mass.) is a 444-bed hospital whose modern computer system explicitly recognizes the need to confront cost reduction. At the heart of the system is an emphasis on determining standard costs for each test and procedure.

Manhattan Eye, Ear and Throat Hospital (New York, N.Y.), a 150-bed specialized surgical hospital, is in the early stages of installing an integrated system to computerize all phases of its operation. The new system will incorporate a variety of features that increase efficiency and reduce costs.

Hospital Corporation of America (Nashville, Tenn.), the leading operator of proprietary hospitals, uses computer systems not only to improve management and efficiency, but also to cope with the new health care environment.

Common Experience

Clearly, there are major differences among the hospitals interviewed—in size, mission, extent of computerization, types of systems installed in the past, and strategies for future efforts. Nevertheless, there are at least four types of common experience that require emphasis.

Aggressive effort to improve systems. Each freestanding hospital, along with the giant HCA organization, was engaged in a major effort to modernize and/or extend its computerization system. Even the two hospitals with the most advanced systems, University Hospital and Beth

Israel, were in the process of improving their systems and increasing the scope of applications.

Emphasis on cost reduction. All interviewed hospital executives emphasized the reduction of operating costs as a major managerial objective. With the single exception of NYU Hospital, all executives interviewed expressed concern regarding the problems of operating under the new prospective payment rules and were cognizant of the need to develop computer-assisted arrangements for reviewing length of patient stay and for eliminating unnecessary procedures.

Aggressive professional management. In each organization the executives in charge of computerization efforts were found to be relatively young persons who were well trained and experienced. In six of the eight organizations the chief information services executives had systems experience in industry. All appeared to be abreast of the latest technology and to be committed to attaining high levels of computerization within their organizations.

Substantial budget. Each organization appeared to be operating under a very substantial budget for data processing. Admittedly, exact amounts were disclosed in only a few interviews, but in no instance was financial hardship mentioned as a principal constraint in expanding systems.

The Pace of New Adoptions

Needless to say, no hard and fast estimates can be made as to how rapidly U.S. hospitals will move to implement a broad range of applications in, say, the next five years. But three general observations drawn from the interviews and the literature can provide a general assessment of the likely pace of adoption: U.S. hospitals taken as a whole have not yet advanced very far in applying new era technology to their operations; the forces propelling adoptions are quite strong and show no signs of weakening; and a number of factors, including costs, resistance to change, and problems of implementation, have served to slow down the pace of adoption and are likely to continue to do so in the years ahead.

The Unfinished Agenda

Regarding the first observation, there is evidence in Table 3.2 as well as in the interview material that the majority of U.S. hospitals have not yet advanced beyond utilization of computers for financial operations, patient admissions, and limited applications in medical records and DRG analysis. Moreover, as noted earlier, patient billings, accounts receivable, and general ledger applications appear to be largely carried out with old-era technology and still await integration with other applications.

But the most important finding from the interviews and the literature is that most hospitals, large and small, have not yet moved toward integrated systems linked by telecommunication networks, in which users are able to draw upon or contribute to data bases in order to assist with operational or managerial problems. Table 3.2 indicates a rapid increase in use of order entry systems (from 13.0 percent to 40.4 percent from 1981 to 1984), but many of these systems are quite limited in function and are even more limited in the extent to which they permit retrieval of information. For the most part, hospitals have simply not yet entered into the stage of data-base applications. Moreover, among those that have, such as University Hospital, very few have even begun to make much use of distributed systems to draw upon stored information for managerial and clinical decisionmaking. Thus, in this regard widespread adoption of totally integrated systems, in which all activities have access to a common data base, lies some years ahead, probably in the 1990s, because vendors are still developing the necessary hardware and software.[18]

This, of course, raises the question of how far hospitals, especially smaller hospitals, will need to go in installing modern systems before they are adequately equipped. Here again, no certain conclusions can be drawn, but there are good reasons to argue that virtually all hospitals will ultimately find it necessary to operate some sort of in-house integrated data base system or be linked to such a system as part of a larger organizational arrangement. The need for historical and other comparative information to provide standards for monitoring patient care costs under prospective payment arrangements would appear to be the most immediate and compelling reason for installing systems equipped to collect and archive detailed clinical and cost information that can be retrieved and analyzed. But a second reason can be found in the movement toward total health care arrangements in which hospitals become a part (perhaps the focal point) of an extended organization including clinics, physicians' offices, home care delivery systems, and so on. Under such arrangements the hospital must be linked to the other organizations and share a common data base for patient registration, treatment, and billing. Finally, as was well established at Beth Israel Hospital, a sharing of data-base clinical information can be of major importance for treatment.[19] Such usage will tend to be most important in teaching hospitals but should in time prove to be a valuable resource in hospitals everywhere.

Forces Propelling Adoptions

The forces propelling adoptions are essentially of two sorts: pressure to reduce costs to meet competition and to cope with the demands of the new prospective payment arrangements and the nature of the technology and the rate of its development. The first, the pressure to adopt, has been treated previously; the second, technology, requires discussion.

One of the striking findings of this study is that it is possible for each hospital to proceed along its own path toward a wider range of applications. The technology is extremely flexible in the sense that applications can be made incrementally. Stand-alone applications of small systems are feasible in a large number of operations. Old- and new-era technology can be wedded, and small systems can be linked to form large systems. This is, indeed, the principal way in which the new technology is being put into place. Such flexibility can be enormously helpful in permitting management to proceed within the limitations of its financial and human resources (although, as we shall see, it poses problems).

The other point to make regarding technology is, of course, that it is moving forward extremely rapidly. New applications are being of-fered—as well as new ways of carrying out old applications—and typically at lower prices and with fewer problems than formerly in terms of installation and operations.

A number of important new applications are in the wings. For example, the portable bedside terminal that monitors a number of aspects of the patient's condition in the hospital, in an intermediate care facility, or in the home is already available, although it has as yet found only limited use. More distant in terms of market availability but already well advanced in terms of development in the engineering stage are optical data storage and other developments that promise to revolutionize the archiving of data and to accelerate the movement toward utilizing large integrated data-base systems.

Constraints and Obstacles

Constraints on the pace of bringing in the new systems are likely to arise because of investment costs, managerial skepticism and resistance, and delays in implementation.

Investment costs. In making investment decisions modern businesses typically follow a procedure requiring that the expected benefits of the capital improvement, measured in terms of reduced cost or increased profitability (from new products, etc.) exceed the expected costs, measured in terms of the costs of capital (i.e., capital recovery and interest). In contrast, for more than a decade U.S. hospitals have operated under an arrangement in which estimated depreciation (the year's appropriate share of the original cost of equipment assuming a given expected "life") is charged to third-party payers as an "extra" on hospital billings. This is commonly known as a capital recovery charge or "pass-through" and makes it possible for hospitals to install equipment without justifying the expenditure on the basis of reduction in operating costs or of increased revenues.[20] Curiously, this provision does not appear to have played a major role in facilitating computerization. In discussions with hospital managers the pass-through provision was mentioned only twice, yet the possibility of direct operational savings through computerization was noted in every interview. Nevertheless, for a decade or more hospital expenditures for high technology diagnostic and treatment equipment and for buildings have to a large extent been made possible by such capital recovery provisions.[21]

Why capital expenditures for new technology have not been regarded in the same light as those for diagnostic and treatment equipment is not clear. It seems likely that top management and hospital boards have found little reason to press for cost reduction under the old retrospective payment arrangement, have been skeptical of the possibilities for improving the quality of health care through use of computer systems, and have been reluctant to tackle the problems inherent in moving into new and untried modes of operation. At the same time, the gains in quality of health care from acquisition of clinical equipment have been stressed by medical staff. If this is the case, capital recovery pass-throughs could play a more important role in computerization as management faces the challenges of a changed environment.

It is by no means certain, however, that the current arrangements for capital recovery will be available in the years ahead. The pass-through provision has been continued provisionally under the new Medicare payment arrangements, but more than a year ago Congress appointed a committee to study alternatives. No findings have as yet been brought in, but one proposal under serious consideration is to simply increase DRG allowances by a fixed percentage markup for all hospitals rather than to allow specific pass-throughs. Such an arrangement would ignore differences in past capital expenditures by hospitals, would put an end to this special incentive for further investment, and would place hospitals in the position of having to justify capital expenditures on a return-on-investment basis.[22]

Under the flat rate arrangement, investment cost becomes an important but not necessarily prohibitive constraint. Significant modernization and expansion of systems are essential for the information and cost controls needed to cope with the new emphasis on cost reduction. The gains from computerization are likely to lie not so much in direct labor savings (although these are important) as in the indirect savings made possible by more careful budgeting and control of departmental operations and in the contributions that increased availability of financial and clinical information can make to the efficient and effective treatment of patients. Under conditions of intense competition and prospective payment, the investment decision rests not so much on the question "How much direct savings does the new system make possible?" as on "How can we survive if we do not get our house in order?" The answer to the latter question may well be that the benefits of modernization are the losses prevented in the future.

Yet this argument does not obviate the fact that computerization will have to compete with high technology clinical equipment for the investment dollar. In a highly competitive marketplace many new capital-intensive medical technologies, including surgical lasers, kidney stone lithotreptors, magnetic resonance imaging, and ultrasound diagnosis of vascular disorders, can go far to attract patients.[23] To the extent that capital budgets are allocated to such equipment, less funding is available for computer hardware and software, and the pace of computerization is slowed.

Resistance to change. U.S. hospitals have, for the most part, been conservatively managed. Except in the case of profit-making hospitals, management has not been motivated to reduce costs in order to generate profits. Moreover, retrospective payment arrangements have discouraged efforts to increase operating efficiency. The result is that in today's changed environment, many heads of hospitals and their boards tend to be poorly informed regarding the new technology, skeptical that it will improve the quality of care, and loathe to "venture into the unknown" and take on the difficult tasks of deciding what technology to employ, purchasing equipment and software, retraining personnel, and putting the organization through the trying experience of shakedown.

This resistance is reinforced by the tradition or "culture" of the medical staff itself, particularly in view of the fact that some of the leading physicians will play a major role in the management of the hospital. In general, doctors share a view that maintenance of the quality of medical care is the overriding objective in the operation of the hospital and that an increasing emphasis on cost control is likely to erode standards of practice. Moreover, they tend to resist efforts to standardize procedures. Given such a value system they are likely to resist many of the changes inherent in putting modern systems into place.

Moreover, the wide range of systems and vendors has from the outset presented hospitals with a bewildering array of options. The rapid rate of improvement in systems and the continually declining costs of hardware often suggest that delay may bring better opportunities. Clearly, these characteristics of the advance of technology have frequently been the cause of delays in decisions to modernize.[24]

Problems in implementing the new systems. Unfortunately, the decision to install a new system and purchase the necessary hardware does not bring the system into full and effective operation. Software must be designed, personnel must be trained to operate the system, and, finally, the staff must accept the superiority of the new technology over older methods and utilize the new resource fully. It is clear from the interview evidence that software design, training, and the process of gaining acceptance have acted to slow down significantly the pace of implementation in the past and are likely to continue to do so in the years ahead. Software design poses a major problem in introducing new systems except in instances where turnkey systems are adopted. Even here modifications are likely to be required. Most of the hospital executives interviewed found it necessary to bring in consultants to work with in-house personnel, and all experienced major delays. In the case of one large medical center, the writer learned that the contracting supplier of a major administrative system proved unable to complete the design of software and to put in place the system ordered.

Training also was found to involve a lengthy and demanding effort in every hospital studied. For example, at Beth Israel training of personnel for the planned data base materials management system scheduled to be installed in the early summer of 1986 had already begun at the time of interview (May 1985).

Finally, acceptance of the new systems and a willingness to utilize them fully were major problems, at least among certain personnel. The difficulty appears to arise mainly among managers and physicians. In none of the hospitals had there been more than limited application of the system's capability for planning purposes. The author was told by a leading medical economist that in one major medical center (not interviewed), perhaps the most advanced in the country in terms of sophistication of its systems, it had taken ten years for top management to get department heads to use their computer systems for budgeting procedures!

Similarly, physicians have in many instances been slow to fully utilize hospital information systems. Where such systems are installed, doctors for the most part continue to rely on nurses to enter orders. Moreover, there does not appear as yet to be any strong demand for improving access to the system by installing a larger number of terminals in doctors' lounges and offices.

The Outlook

Costs are likely to continue to impede the rate of adoption, and given less favorable capital recovery provisions and the need for larger systems, the years ahead are likely to bring greater problems of funding than have been faced thus far. Problems of implementation are, of course, inherent in the task of putting new systems into place; and the requirements for training a large number of personnel, designing software for larger and more complex systems, and instituting the necessary organizational changes will bring major challenges to management.

Yet resistance to change is being eroded bit by bit by the successful experience of the more progressive hospitals, and the confusion that attends a rapidly changing technology is likely to subside as the merits of the various vendors' offerings become more generally understood. These constraints will probably continue to retard progress, but it seems unlikely that they will play as great a role in the future as in the past. Because the slow dissipation of managerial ignorance, skepticism, and inertia has marked the introduction of new technology throughout modern history, it would be surprising if a similar process of changing attitudes were not at work in the adoption of computerization technology by U.S. hospitals.

Moreover, the forces propelling change are strong indeed. Hospitals simply must accommodate the need to reduce cost and restructure their operations if they are to remain viable. Such accommodation requires utilization of the new systems, especially in the case of coping with DRG.

The prospective payment requirements are new, and their full implications are not yet clear, but studies of early DRG experience in New Jersey, where the regulations were introduced roughly three years earlier than elsewhere, indicate that under pressure to conform to the new regulations hospitals found it necessary from the outset to increase the use of computers and to involve the medical staff in order to comply with the new requirements.[25] Moreover, one of the New Jersey studies indicated that the hospitals that performed most efficiently under the new arrangements had the following characterstics: (1) a hospital-wide training program; (2) a full-time staff member acting as DRG coordinator; (3) a physician DRG committee; (4) an effective data processing system; and (5) some additional staffing.

The lesson of the early New Jersey experience—a lesson strongly supported by most of the interviews, especially the experience at New Hanover Hospital (the only hospital that had operated under DRG at the time of the interview)—is that the move to prospective payment is a major force accelerating the pace of computerization. The early experience with DRG readily makes clear the necessity for employee training and for securing the active involvement of staff physicians.

Taken on balance it seems likely that the pace of adoption will accelerate, not decline. There is one issue, however, that remains unresolved: the extent to which health care services will evolve into very large hospital systems and other health service institutions. The rapid growth of the major for-profit hospital chains has prompted some to predict that the United States is moving toward the creation of ten to fifteen very large systems that would dominate U.S. health care.

But the superior efficiency of for-profit hospitals has by no means been established. Their earlier quite profitable experience was at least partially due to favorable real estate transactions and policies of locating in areas in which demand conditions were favorable. In 1985, the vulnerability of these hospitals to new environmental conditions was demonstrated by the heavy losses of the largest chain, HCA.

What seems well established is that there is a strong tendency for the development of new cooperative arrangements among some hospitals (for example, the joining together of some Catholic-sponsored hospitals to effect economies through specialization and the sharing of resources), the creation of joint arrangements between hospitals and other health services, and a general tendency for individual hospitals to become more specialized and to downsize their operations. In each of these trends the new technology is likely to play a major role.

Computerization and Work

It was noted earlier that in coping with increased competition and the requirements of prospective payment a two-pronged strategy must be pursued. One line of attack focuses on gaining greater control of the protocols followed in treating patients; the other, on increased efforts to reduce costs and increase productivity in all departments. Most hospitals are likely to emphasize the first approach initially as management attempts to attack directly the costs associated with each patient's treatment by reducing patient stays and eliminating unneeded tests, procedures, and medications.

But ultimately there must be a major effort to root out inefficiency wherever it is found. Such an effort will be driven by an increasing need to reduce costs in any form, but it also will be dictated by the logic of the kind of systems required to cope with prospective payment management. Hospitals simply cannot proceed far toward controlling costs on a case-by-case basis without computer systems that merge financial and clinical data and process such information without the delays necessitated by old time paper-pushing techniques. Such systems also will eliminate routine chores, provide the financial and clerical information to reduce costs by monitoring vendor performance and securing the best prices and terms, control inventories to reduce carrying charges, improve collections and cash management, and reduce maintenance and housekeeping budgets through better planning and more careful control of operations. Thus, the impact of computerization on work is broad indeed and touches a wide range of activities throughout the hospital. The impact of computerization on employment can be divided into three categories: displacement effects, changing nature of work, and career opportunities.

Displacement Effects

It is likely that the immediate displacement effects of computerization will be confined to low-level clerical personnel and will not be large. Although the total volume of paperwork generated by all personnel, including professional and technical personnel, is very large indeed, the share of total hospital employment accounted for by clerical personnel alone is relatively small, probably no more than 15 percent in most hospitals (somewhat below the average for the nation and well below the typical share among such service organizations as government, banking, and insurance).[26] Moreover, the number of clerical personnel engaged principally in routine "paper factory" types of operations— workers whose major work assignments can be readily appropriated by the computer— is considerably less, with the remainder scattered through the organization as secretaries and clerical assistants. Based on the interview evidence it seems reasonable to assume that direct and immediate displacement effects will be small and confined to some fraction of these workers in very routine repetitive jobs such as posting entries in patient billings, payroll, and purchasing.[27]

But the longer run effects are likely to be somewhat more substantial for two reasons. The first is that work can be reorganized to take advantage of the fact that personnel are being relieved of time-consuming routine chores. Where computers take over or assist in the scheduling of beds, nursing duties, patient visits to radiology and physical therapy, or in the preparation of menus, charges for various procedures and medications, and a host of other tasks, work is abridged. New work will undoubtedly arise, but the opportunity to reorganize work and to operate the hospital on a leaner staff would appeal to cost-conscious management.

The second reason is that the increased reliance on computerization to reduce patient stays and eliminate unnecessary procedures and medication results in a larger ratio of patients to staff. Here once again the staff is leaner. When patient load increases the hospital is able to operate without proportional increases in employment; when patient load decreases, as is currently the trend, staff will tend to shrink.

Computerization and Changes
in the Nature of Work

In previous chapters I demonstrated that computerization can eliminate tedious, repetitive chores such as posting or transcribing data and also can eliminate or simplify complex tasks such as scheduling or preparing reports drawn from multiple data sources. Moreover, computerization facilitates more sophisticated analyses than were previously possible and thereby enhances the quality of patient treatment and of management. Given these capabilities and the fact that computerization is applicable throughout the hospital, computerization must inexorably alter the nature of almost all work to a greater or lesser extent. The interviews and literature provided relatively little specific information regarding changes in the nature of work, but they did shed some light on several occupations.

Clerical personnel. All managers interviewed agreed that computerization eliminates certain routine clerical chores and alters the work content of those persons affected; new work is often somewhat broader in scope and involves a higher level of responsibility. For example, clerks shifted from posting chores to handling customer or payer queries become responsible for dealing with a wider range of problems than previously encountered and must be more familiar with hospital policies and procedures. Managers did not feel, however, that present personnel in low-level assignments were unable to handle the new tasks, although there was a (contradictory) majority opinion that management would probably be more selective in future hiring.

It is not clear how the work of other clericals throughout the hospital is being altered by computerization, partly because hospitals are in the midst of change and the results are not yet apparent and partly because other factors are present. As an example of the latter, one clerical position that is becoming more demanding is medical records clerk. Yet the upgrading of this position is more a result of DRG reporting requirements than it is a function of computerization.

Many of the remaining clerical tasks are as yet untouched by computerization or are affected only marginally. In response to questions regarding the effect of computerization on clerks handling stock and preparing carts in the pharmacy department at HCA's Westside Hospital, the author was advised that computerization would make their work simpler and "permit them to do a better job." Yet these jobs will surely be impacted in time. For example, the reduction of recordkeeping and invoice preparation and the closer control of inventories through on-line ordering-reporting systems with vendors such as the American Hospital Supply Company may be expected to bring about new duties and responsibilities for those employed in hospital supply. There will be less clerical work but more monitoring of the total purchasing system, more information available for planning, and stricter requirements that purchasing and inventory levels be managed to bring costs to optimum levels.

Managerial personnel. Computerization is just beginning to affect management. The interviews revealed only scattered use of microcomputers for managerial planning and control and indicated that much of management's time is spent in selecting new systems or putting them into operation. Moreover, few hospitals yet have the systems necessary to accumulate the clinical and financial information necessary to carry out effective utilization review, analyze case mix, or vigorously reduce departmental costs through analysis of variances from standard costs. Yet the pressure is on, and the direction of movement is clear.

Traditionally, an emphasis on professional management has not been widespread in U.S. hospitals. The number of managers relative to other occupations has been relatively small, and under old-time retrospective payment arrangements, managerial authority and scope of action have been limited.[28] Yet both the interviews and the literature indicated that hospitals are moving toward more aggressive management in their efforts to reduce costs. It is arguable that such an emphasis on tighter control may in certain ways conflict with the efforts of physicians to provide the highest possible level of medical care, but there is little doubt that the pressure to manage more closely will continue and that computerization will increasingly support this effort.

Nursing personnel. In addition to direct patient care, nurses perform a variety of duties, including maintaining a current account of the patient's treatment and condition, answering telephone queries, scheduling patient treatment in ancillary departments, and carrying out administrative tasks such as scheduling and supervising other nurses.

The potential for reducing nursing clerical chores on the floor may be large because nurses on patient duty were reported to be spending more than 40 percent of their time on clerical chores. This potential, however, will be difficult to realize fully for several reasons. In many systems nurses are responsible for entering doctors' orders into the computer and even when nurses record information for their own use in computerized form, the required information must be transferred from notes to the computer. Moreover, very few hospitals as yet make use of bedside terminals that permit nurses to directly record information on the patient's condition.

But the technology exists to relieve the nurse of a number of these chores, and in time both doctor and nurse will come to rely heavily on the terminal to record and retrieve information. In the meanwhile, well- designed hospital information systems are reducing the time spent in a variety of tasks such as answering phones, placing orders, determining test results, and preparing medication schedules. In addition, the ready availability of results from ancillary departments makes possible more professional nursing.

Where nurses are engaged in scheduling and preparing administrative reports, the computer can frequently provide substantial assistance. These tasks in the past have required a good measure of skill and judgment and have commanded prestige and superior pay. In the short run there may be problems in transferring nurses from these tasks to regular duties. During a longer period adjustments of duties can be effected, and the entire nursing unit can perform more effectively and at lower cost per patient.

An additional observation is that there is virtually no limit to the clinical information that can be made immediately accessible to nurses by sophisticated data base systems, permitting them to determine proper protocols for patient care according to specific diagnoses or to cope with emergencies.

Other professionals and technicians. Among ancillary departments computerization is reducing the time spent in performing both clerical and operational tasks. For example, many laboratory procedures are carried out by computer-assisted equipment; results and reports are rendered electronically. At the same time, more sophisticated tests and procedures can be executed and important clinical information can be accessed instantly by professionals or technicians (e.g., the information available on dosages and compatibility of medications as well as the patient's age, diagnosis, allergies, etc., which then are instantly available to the pharmacist). The result is that these personnel are able to perform their responsibilities at a much higher level of professionalism, but more problem-solving and decisionmaking skills are demanded of them.

Computerization and Changing Career Opportunities

Hospitals, of necessity, have always placed a considerable emphasis on credentialing. As a result, career opportunities are restricted by areas of specialization, and opportunities for advancement are relatively limited. Hospitals do not have well-developed internal labor markets. Clerks may not aspire to be laboratory technicians nor laboratory technicians, radiologists—at least not without returning to school for special training. It is unlikely that computerization will alter this situation. In fact the tendency for computerization to upgrade work is likely to promote an even greater tendency toward credentialing.

One change may well lie in the area of management, however. The new stress on professional management is likely to open up new career opportunities because the increased demand for able professionals will in all likelihood bring higher pay and status. Moreover, the career ladders are likely to be longer as larger health delivery organizations come to play a more important role. This was the case in HCA, where young managers enjoyed considerable opportunity for promotion. Yet once again the emphasis is on professionalism. The new managers require special training in hospital administration and/or computer science. It is unlikely that low-rung administrative personnel will find opportunities to advance to the higher ranks. Again, we find that for those with meager educational achievement, computerization limits their opportunities for both entry and advancement.

The Outlook for Employment in Hospitals

The previous sections have focused narrowly on the direct effects of computerization on work and career opportunities, but the changes that are forthcoming are likely to be more profound than those described because they are influenced by other forces as well. Under the reimbursement procedures that obtained until the 1980s, hospitals were able to operate without cost controls and to increase employment rapidly and without careful regard for the need to maximize productivity per worker. Now, with greater competition from other health institutions and rising pressure for cost containment, employment is being reduced. The year 1983 saw the first small decrease, but the years ahead promise significant further decreases. In a carefully documented analysis, Howard Berliner pointed to a number of factors that are likely to bring reductions in hospital employment,[29] among which are pressures on hospitals to reduce costs brought about by changing reimbursement arrangements, pressures from employers and third-party payers, the shift toward ambulatory surgery and outpatient care, and new labor-saving medical technology. Berliner also noted the declining importance of public hospitals with their high employment-per-bed ratios and the rising importance of multihospital arrangements and for-profit hospitals, which are characterized by low relative employment levels.

These trends toward reduced employment are accompanied by a changing composition of employment.[30] In general, the trends are toward a greater use of professionals and a lesser use of relatively untrained personnel. With physicians in markedly greater supply, physician extenders are no longer in demand. Registered nurses are increasingly being used to substitute for less flexible licensed practical nurses. Technologists, rather than technicians, are being retrained to cope with the changing requirements of medical technology. Workers at the lower end of the spectrum of health personnel—nurses aides, orderlies, attendants— appear to be the most expendable as hospitals seek to reduce labor costs, retrench in terms of number of beds, and shift their focus toward the treatment of more acutely ill patients.

Finally, there are a large number of employees in hospitals that are not classified as health service employees—managers, nonhealth professionals, and clerical personnel along with a host of lower-level maintenance and janitorial personnel, food service and laundry workers, and the like. Managers and clerical workers already have been considered in the earlier analysis of the impact of computerization. They are among those most directly impacted by technology, but their employment also will be strongly affected by the more general trend toward cost containment and reorganization. Here again, those with the higher levels of skills and training are most protected in the changing hospital labor market. Managers will continue to be in demand to cope with the complex problems of reorganizing and rendering more efficient the complex administrative machinery of hospitals. But at the lower end of the nonhealth service staffs, a general move to reverse earlier tendencies is likely to bring about a tightening of work assignments, a reduction of employment, and some shift to part-time work.

One point remains to be considered: the offsetting effects of an expansion of institutional arrangements other than hospitals. It seems likely that many jobs lost through hospital retrenchment and cost containment will be regained through job openings in the expanding segments. Yet the shift in employment can be no more than partial. To the extent that employment is reduced because of the introduction of technology, elimination of unneeded workers, or rearrangement of work, there is no reason to expect that these jobs will reappear elsewhere.

Notes

1. American Hospital Association, *Hospital Statistics* (Chicago: AHA, 1984 edition), p. 4, and Department of Commerce, *Statistical Abstract of the United States, 1984* (Washington, D.C.: GPO, 1985–86), pp. 106, 493.

2. J.C. Goldsmith, "The Changing Role of the Hospital," in Eli Ginzberg, ed., *The U.S. Health Care System: A Look to the 1990s* (Totowa, N.J.: Rowman & Allanheld, 1985), p. 49.

3. Ibid., p. 52.

4. Ibid, p. 55.

5. The definitions that follow are drawn principally from Lawrence D. Brown, "The Managerial Imperative and Organizational Innovation", in Ginzberg, *The U.S. Health Care System*, pp. 30–35. The definition of voluntary hospital organizations comes from Howard Berliner, *Employment in the U.S. Health Care Delivery Sector,* Report submitted to the U.S. Office of Technology Assessment, October 1984, pp. 10–11.

Health Maintenance Organizations (HMOs) are organizational arrangements in which the financing and delivery of care are combined by the integration of prepayment and group practices. Subscribers pay monthly fixed premiums to the plan, which acts as an insurer. Physicians and hospitals are its principal providers, each operating on a negotiated fee arrangement.

Voluntary Hospital Organizations are multi-institutional systems in which individual hospitals have banded together to effect economies and improved services for any of a number of reasons, including the sharing of clinical services, managerial services, and data processing systems, economies in purchasing, easier access to capital markets, and a rationalization of employment patterns.

Preferred Provider Organizations (PPOs) are fee-for- service groups of physicians and/or hospitals that contract with a third-party payer, such as a self-insured company or trust fund, to provide services at a predetermined, usually discounted, price. Patients are usually enrolled by third-party insurers, such as Blue Cross, and may elect (at extra cost) to choose physicians other than preferred providers.

Ambulatory Surgical Centers (ASCs) are facilities that provide ambulatory surgery without the formal entry arrangements of ordinary hospitals and, of course, without the patient remaining overnight or longer. ASCs may be freestanding or attached to a hospital.

For-Profit Hospitals are hospitals (mostly chains) that are owned by stockholders and that commit part of their revenues as dividends. The major multihospital for-profit organizations are made up largely of community nonprofit hospitals that have been purchased. In addition, for-profit hospital organizations, such as the Hospital Corporation of America, operate a number of nonprofit hospitals on a fee basis.

6. Under the new DRG procedures hospitals are not only required to submit a statement of procedures and costs for each patient but must submit at frequent intervals (typically about every three weeks) to a detailed examination of a number of patients' records as selected by an outside Peer Review Board.

7. Medical records must be retained for long periods of time both for reference in the subsequent treatment of a patient and for possible use in the event of liability suits.

8. Blue Cross–Blue Shield of Greater New York, *Hospital Information System Vendor Survey 1982–1983*, Vol. 1 (New York: BC–BS, 1983) p. 36.

9. The text of the report states that "the set of functions identified in each application is not necessarily exhaustive, but reflects what is considered the important majority." Ibid., p. 35. As a matter of fact, the list is now out of date and incomplete. Not listed are a number of computerized functions that include several related to DRG analysis.

10. See Michael Nathanson, "'90s Will Herald in Integrated Systems," *Modern Healthcare*, August 1, 1984, p. 86.

11. Order entry systems provide for terminal entry and telecommunications transfer of physician orders to ancillary departments. Often, but not always, the system allows departments to report results on tests and procedures. Although order entry systems for the most part employ new-era hardware and software, highly effective but expensive patient care systems with order entry and reporting

capability (like airline reservation systems) were introduced more than fifteen years ago.

12. Michael Nathanson, "Hospitals Pump Dollars into Finance, Nursing," *Modern Healthcare*, September 1984, pp. 114–123.

13. Nathanson, "'90s Will Herald in Integrated Systems."

14. Nathanson, "Hospitals Pump Dollars into Finance, Nursing," p. 114.

15. Here again the precedent is well established in industry. Individual departments examine differences between budgeted and actual costs in light of the actual product (procedure) mix, valued on the basis of standard costs determined by industrial engineers.

16. See Sheldon I. Dorenfest, "Computers Can Figure Out DRGs If You Can Figure Out Computer Market," *Modern Healthcare*, February 2, 1984, p. 135.

17. Address requests to T.M. Stanback, Jr., Conservation of Human Resources, Columbia University, 2880 Broadway, N.Y., N.Y. 10025.

18. Nathanson, "'90s Will Herald in Integrated Systems," p. 86.

19. Howard L. Bleich, et al., "Clinical Computing in a Teaching Hospital," *The New England Journal of Medicine*, March 21, 1985, pp. 756–764.

20. This provision does not completely enable the hospital to recoup the cost of new hardware because only the purchase price is recovered and the recovery takes place during the depreciation life of the asset. Interest costs of any debt incurred must be met out of the hospital's regular charges.

21. Hospitals must obtain a certification from state authorities that the installation is appropriate and needed, but apparently, such certification has not proven to be a problem in adopting new systems. The pass-through does not apply to expenditures for software or additional required personnel, although these, too, may be recovered where retrospective payment schemes still obtain.

22. The current capital recovery pass-through provisions are similar in effect to the investment credit provisions of the tax law that allow private sector firms to recover a part of the cost of capital through tax reductions.

23. Wayne I. Roe, "Medical Technology Under PPS: An Uncertain Future," *Hospitals*, January 16, 1985, p. 88.

24. A case in point was the recent announcement by IBM that it was about to unveil its first new accounting software package in a decade. Many hospitals delayed purchases of software until they had an opportunity to determine the merits of the new IBM offering. Nathanson, "Hospitals Pump Dollars into Finance, Nursing," p. 114.

25. Jeffrey Wasserman, *DRG Evaluation, Volume 1, Introduction and Overview* (Princeton, N.J.: Health Research and Educational Trust of N.J., 1982).

26. The latest estimates available from Deparment of Labor statistics are for the year 1978 and probably overstate the percentages of clerical labor today. In 1978, the shares of total employment accounted for by clerical workers were 16.12 percent in hospitals, 26.81 percent in universities and colleges, 21.54 percent in government, 64.48 percent in banking, 45.42 percent in insurance, and 17.91 percent in all industries. U.S. Bureau of Labor Statistics, *The National Industry-Occupation Employment Matrix, 1970, 1978, and Projected 1990*, Bulletin 2086, April 1981.

27. New Hanover Memorial Hospital projected a reduction of only twenty-two workers (all clerical) out of a total of more than 1,700 as a result of its new health information system.

28. The percentage of total hospital employment accounted for by managers, officials, and proprietors in 1978 was 3.10 compared to 9.68 in local public administration, 28.84 in banking, 12.08 in insurance, and 10.71 in total U.S. employment.

29. Berliner, *Employment in the Health Care Delivery Sector*, Chapter 1.

30. For an excellent discussion of this subject, see ibid., Chapter 2.

4

Computerization in
Universities and Colleges

Universities and colleges, like the New York City government and
U.S. hospitals generally, are facing major difficulties in their efforts to
provide services under financial stress. They differ, however, in that they
have not had thrust upon them mandates that place heavy emphasis
on new applications of computer and related technology as a means of
solving their problems. Moreover, universities and colleges face a somewhat different sort of challenge. Demands for applications of the new
technology are occurring on two fronts: academic computing, which
supports the basic operational missions of teaching and research, and
administrative computing, which assists administration and management.
Each poses special problems, and each, to some extent, competes with
the other for resources.

This chapter is based on interviews with administrators of four
institutions of higher education: Stevens Institute of Technology, Iona
College, Columbia University, and New York University. A detailed case
study of one of these institutions, Stevens Institute, is contained in
Appendix C. Six sections follow. The first reviews the major problems
currently facing institutions of higher education. The second and third
address the nature of academic computerization (teaching, research, and
library operation) and administrative computerization respectively. The
fourth briefly describes the four institutions interviewed. The fifth and
sixth sections assess the outlook for academic and administrative computing in the years immediately ahead and the implications for work
and employment opportunities.

Higher Education at the Crossroads

U.S. universities and colleges today face mounting pressures from
declining enrollments, rising costs, and declining governmental support,

which have resulted in increased competition among institutions for students and a growing need to raise tuition and other student fees. Behind the decline in enrollments is the aging of the baby boom generation. The total number of eighteen-year olds reached its peak in 1979 and the number of eighteen- to twenty-four-year olds in 1981.[1] Enrollment in both public and private institutions peaked in the fall of 1983, and projections as far ahead as 1993 promise continual declines.[2] Rising costs have placed a heavy burden on all institutions, particularly since the late 1970s, with increases exceeding the rate of inflation (see Table 4.1).

In the face of these pressures, universities and colleges have experienced declining governmental support and have been forced to look increasingly to other sources of income. This can readily be seen in a comparison of the distribution of revenue sources in all institutions for the academic years of 1981-1982 and 1971-1972 (Table 4.2).[3] In recent years, pressures have mounted. Until the fall of 1981, increases in tuition and student fees had, on average, been held to levels below those of the cost of living index, but since that date they have risen each year by 3 to 8 percent in excess of the index.[4] Moreover, many private institutions, particularly those hard hit by declines in governmental support and a shift of enrollments to public institutions where tuitions are far lower, have been faced with the alternatives of substantial increases in tuition, retrenchment, consolidation with other schools, or closure.[5] Public institutions, although less critically affected, also have experienced increasing difficulties.

Within this environment universities and colleges must cope with the challenge of making greater use of the new computer technology. On the one hand, computerization offers the promise of more effective teaching and research, improvement in ability to recruit, and greater administrative and managerial efficiency. On the other hand, the new technology requires heavy expenditures and necessitates organizational change.

Academic Computing: The Challenge of the New Technology

Computers have played a major role in research in the sciences, engineering, mathematics, and in certain social sciences. In other disciplines, however, especially in the humanities, technology has played only a minor role. In these latter areas, research does not require complex analysis of data but rather access to bibliographic, textual, or other information (frequently from a variety of sources) and the ability to examine, analyze, and write about these materials. Only in recent years

TABLE 4.1
Consumer and Higher Education Price Indexes,[a] 1979-1980 to 1983-1984

Price Indexes	1979-1980 to 1983-1984 (percentage change)
Inflation index	31.1
Higher education price indexes	
All expenditures	36.6
Professional salaries	32.2
Nonprofessional salaries	31.3
Fringe benefits	54.8

[a] Price indexes adjusted for academic year.

Source: V. W. Plisko and J. D. Stern, *The Condition of Education* (Washington, D.C.: National Center for Educational Statistics, 1985 edition), p. 118, and U.S. Department of Commerce, *Statistical Abstract of the United States, 1984* (Washington, D.C.: GPO, 1985-1986), p. 155.

TABLE 4.2
Distribution of Revenue Sources, 1971-1972 and 1981-1982 (percentages)

| | 1971-1972 | | 1981-1982 | |
Sources	Public	Private	Public	Private
Government[a]	62.5	24.9	57.6	19.9
Private sources	2.6	10.3	3.2	9.2
Student-related sources[b]				
Tuition, fees	13.1	35.4	13.0	36.8
Auxiliary enterprises[c]	13.2	14.4	11.8	12.0
Institutional[d]	8.6	15.0	14.5	22.2

[a] Includes appropriations, grants and contracts but excludes direct federal aid to students.
[b] Includes federal aid to students (e.g., Pell grants).
[c] Includes revenues generated by operations, such as residence halls, food services.
[d] Includes endowment income.

Source: V. W. Plisko and J. D. Stern, *The Condition of Education* (Washington, D.C.: National Center for Educational Statistics, 1985 edition).

has computer-oriented technology offered major research support in the humanities. In teaching, technology also has played a relatively minor role except in laboratory sciences, computer science, and econometrics. For the most part teaching has followed the time-honored mode of classroom instruction, assigned reading of texts or library materials, and limited assignment of papers.

Only recently have technological developments become available to support the instructional process by facilitating the student's library research and out-of-class preparation, or by providing computer-centered supplements or alternatives to lectures. Since the mid-1970s, efforts have been made by a number of institutions to apply computer technology to the academic missions of research and instruction. Yet the results of these efforts are not readily apparent to the casual observer even on the campuses of major universities, except for sharp increases in the number of students enrolled in computer science, a new orientation toward computer use in advanced business administration courses, and a more widespread utilization of computer resources among faculty and graduate students.

The recent advances in technology that are most important for academic applications are as yet not widely publicized. They lie in four major areas: (1) the application of computers and telecommunications to library operations; (2) the increased availability of on-line retrieval services; (3) the movement to network campuses and make computer workstations available to all students and faculty; and (4) the adaptations of new technology to teaching. The first two represent a quiet revolution on the U.S. college campus. Most libraries have already moved a considerable distance toward applying the new technology internally and toward utilizing on-line retrieval services in their own operations. Libraries and/or computer service centers are increasingly making on-line data base retrieval services available to students and faculty. The last two are as yet pioneer efforts of a small number of institutions, but these efforts have been widely recognized by other universities and colleges and are generally better known to the public at large.

Libraries and On-line Retrieval Services

Libraries stand at the center of the effort of universities and colleges to apply modern technology to the mission of higher education. Yet less than a decade ago a survey of computer utilization in U.S. higher education indicated that library applications were among those least frequently adopted.

The explanation for this paradox lies in the fact that old-style batch processing through computer centers was applicable to relatively few library operations, whereas modern on-line data-base technology coupled with the availability of new institutional arrangements and commercial services make it possible to bring technology to all of the major functions carried out within the university or college library and to dramatically broaden the range of information services offered to the user.

A brief sketch of principal library functions. It is helpful to examine the major activities performed within the library—acquisition, cataloging, circulation, and reference—and to note how each function is being affected by technology. Acquisition constitutes a major problem for libraries. Because at best only a fraction of the materials available (both new and old) can be purchased within budget constraints, decisions must be made as to what to purchase in light of the library user's needs, the existing collection, and the possibilities of utilizing other collections through interlibrary borrowing. In addition, purchases must be made, deliveries recorded, and payments made.

Closely related to acquisition is the cataloging function—the recording of acquisitions and the maintenance of an inventory. In order that each acquisition may be filed properly and subsequently retrieved and in order that the librarian and user will have available all necessary information on acquisitions, cataloging involves coding the item and describing it in terms of subject, title, author, publisher, and so on. A particularly difficult aspect of this function is keeping track of serial materials that are continually updated.

A third area of responsibility is circulation. Essentially, this is an inventory control function, but unlike business inventory control it involves checking materials out and in, issuing notices of overdue books, and collecting fines.

The fourth major area is reference. In the past this activity involved searching the card catalog, serials catalog, and a variety of published indexes of books, titles, news stories, and abstracts of articles as well as encyclopedia and specialized directories. Although such searches may be carried out by the user, in many instances a skilled reference librarian is called upon for assistance.

How technology is applied. The modern university library can apply on-line data-base technology to each of these areas because modern computers and telecommunications are versatile and a wide variety of data bases, arrangements for cooperation with other libraries, and special services are available. Once an inventory of library holdings is fed into a data base and similar information is available from other university libraries and from the Library of Congress, the library is able to use a computerized system to analyze its holdings, establish criteria for acquisition, consult a list of recommended acquisitions for certain types and levels of libraries, and determine what to acquire. Purchasing is carried out through a terminal with orders transmitted on line to a central computer facility utilized by a large number of libraries.

Cataloging is automated in the modern library. Information to be entered on the catalog card, including coding, is available from the data bases of cooperating libraries or from a special service, and the catalog card is prepared automatically by the service organization and mailed to the library. Only unusual materials need be cataloged within the library.

Bar coding of circulating materials makes it possible to apply on-line data base processing to the circulation function. The circulation desk attendant "wands" the volume and enters the name of the user into the computer which records that the item has been removed and is due back on a given date. The computer issues notices of due dates and fines. Upon return, a similar wanding records that the item has been restored to the collection.

In the automated library, reference services make heavy use of a variety of data bases. If the library's card catalog has been converted to machine readable format (or even where it has been substantially converted, say, for the past several years), the user or librarian can consult a terminal to locate any monograph in the library's collection, determine what journals and serial materials are available, examine indexes to periodicals, or gain access to a wide variety of data bases containing abstracts or even full texts of articles. If, as is likely, the bibliographic search results in requests that materials be made available, the user can determine whether or not the material is in the library's collection (and if so, its availability) and, if necessary, request an interlibrary loan. The librarian, by consulting a data base, can determine what other library can most conveniently supply the needed material and can arrange for a loan.

The above does not exhaust the ways in which library operations are being facilitated by computerization, however, and even more applications are coming on line. A variety of new technologies are in existence or under development including optical disk storage systems, data compression techniques, solid-state and optical (laser) scanners, electrostatic and laser printers, and digital communications.[6] These advances will permit libraries to store materials and deliver them electronically to users and to share resources with other libraries by transfer of entire texts. Moreover, campus networks and dial-in arrangements are beginning to make it possible to extend library catalog and bibliographic services to terminals or microcomputers in faculty offices, dormitories, and faculty and student homes.

Commercial services and voluntary arrangements. Although the role of data-base computer technology and telecommunications is evident in the foregoing discussion of the modern library, the role of commercial services, consortia, and interlibrary cooperation needs further clarification, for each has seen remarkable development in recent years, and each is playing a vital role. Three firms play a key role in making available on-line retrieval systems: Lockheed Information Service of California Corporation, which markets its software under the name of DIALOG; Systems Development Corporation, with ORBIT; and Bibliographic Retrieval Systems of New York, with BRS.[7] These firms do not create data bases, but, rather, buy them (mostly indexing and abstracting services) and sell access to libraries and other information agencies. In addition, there are other vendors of on-line retrieval services, such as the New York Times Company and the Institute for Scientific Research, that sell their own data bases, although most data bases are handled through middlemen.[8] It is estimated that more than 2,800 data bases are available currently, up from approximately 500 in 1979.[9]

Several other organizations that play a highly important role in offering a variety of systems, such as acquisitions, cataloging, circulation, reference, and access to data bases (including the Library of Congress catalog), are consortia or private sector organizations. OCLC (originally Ohio College Library Center, a consortium, now a private firm) apparently has the largest number of subscribers, including public as well as college and university libraries. Research Libraries Group (RLG) is another major organization; it is a corporation owned by thirty-one major universities and research organizations that offers not only a number of library operations systems but also the Research Libraries Inter Library Loan System (RLIN), a shared resources program whereby member libraries have access to each other's collections and use electronic mail to solve problematic reference questions, exchange development information, and cooperate in other ways. Some other similar organizations are the University of Chicago's Library Data Management System (LDMS), the Northwestern On-Line Total Integrated System (NOTIS), the Washington Library Network (WLN), and BITNET, the scholars network.

Still other cooperative arrangements include a large number of state and regional interlibrary lending networks. Columbia University, for example, is a member of RLIN, the New York State Interlibrary Loan System, the Metropolitan New York Cooperative System (METRO), the Regional Medical Library Network, and the Medical Library Center.[10]

Finally, it must be noted that smaller libraries that do not require or cannot afford the full services of these organizations may make use of their facilities by subscribing or participating on a restricted basis. In short, the vast resources currently assembled are available in whole or in part to virtually all libraries within the nation.

Microcomputers and Networks

At present microcomputers dedicated to academic purposes are located mainly in computer labs where students carry out exercises or complete assignments principally in computer science and business administration courses. But, increasingly, single units or small clusters of microcomputers are located in individual departments where faculty members or graduate students through dial-in arrangements with the school's central computer can gain access to data bases located either on campus or available through the library's or central computer center's external network arrangements.[11]

In recent years a number of institutions have begun to make available scholars' workstations to all students and faculty; these are powerful microcomputers with a wide range of capabilities.[12] With such a work-station the user is able to carry out most routine desk work such as composing letters, sending messages, drawing graphs and charts, looking up information on file, or gaining access to data bases. The workstation screen can be subdivided into "windows" that permit the user to work simultaneously on a number of items. In addition, users can utilize electronic mail, which permits direct communication between students or between students and faculty. An especially promising feature is the opportunity offered scholars to communicate with one another anywhere in the nation through BITNET; they can ask questions, send manuscripts for criticism, or engage in joint research.

New Approaches to Teaching

For decades, television, motion pictures, and slides have facilitated instruction in business, educational institutions, and government, but the mode of presentation was, for the most part, one in which the student played a relatively passive role. In recent years, technology that permits the student to interact with the computer instructor or to become involved actively in experimentation or simulation has been used. Some of the new techniques of computer-aided instruction (CAI) are: "help" systems that make it possible for students to request assistance at any point in the lesson, to be prompted, or to extract explanations of increasing complexity if needed; simulations, in which the student works with models of the phenomenon under study; and intelligent tutors, systems in which the program contains the information to be taught and responds to specific requests from the student or is driven by tutoring/diagnostic rules.[13] Many of the new CAI procedures make use of visual aids provided by optical disks.

The range of applications of this new technology is extremely broad and beyond the scope of this discussion, but several applications illustrate the potential for enriching the educational process.

1. In law, students watch a mock trial and may raise objections at any point. Students are then asked to choose the correct reason for objecting from a list of possible reasons. If the answer is incorrect, the computer explains why.[14]
2. In medicine, students work with tutoring programs in which computers simulate patients with a variety of diseases. Students query the "patient" or order tests and receive answers or test results immediately. Proceeding in this manner students make a diagnosis, which the computer either confirms or denies with an explanation.[15]
3. In music, a workstation facilitates keyboard skills by monitoring the student's progress and signaling mistakes.[16]
4. In engineering, programs demonstrate how the properties of simple systems evolve as progressive complications in design or application arise.[17]

A Vision of the Future

In its report to the university's president, the Columbia University Task Force on Information Processing set forth its "vision of the future," which aptly summarized the potential for academic applications of computer, telecommunications, and related technologies as seen in the mid–1980s.

Our recommendations are based on a vision of the future which includes an unprecedented spectrum of choices for faculty and students. The capabilities of individual microcomputers will offer opportunities for searching the major university collections of the world through a series of hierarchical linkages, beginning with the local institutional catalog. The on-line catalog will be an integrated system containing information on holdings, circulation status, and in-process location of new acquisitions. Document delivery, whether in electronic or hard-copy format, can be ordered electronically for the work-station. Browsing can take place either on-line through records displayed in call number order or by visiting the stacks. It appears likely that the archival medium of the future will be optical disk, which means that a much greater range of published information will be available electronically. It appears highly unlikely that optical disc publication will represent the sole format, but rather that the diverse characteristics of scholarly inquiry will require an equally diverse range of information formats and sources. Individual institutions will continue to build local collections of books and journals to support particular scholarly and instructional strengths with the assurance that lesser used materials are available on demand. Changes in library activities will reflect the changing requirements of scholarly habits influenced by the new technology.

In the same way, from microcomputers located in university offices, dormitories, and home studies, Columbia scholars and students will have access to powerful computing capabilities for a variety of requirements involving quantitative calculations and statistical manipulations of data. Through a series of gateways, problems requiring greater computational capability than available at the microcomputer will be moved to more powerful systems elewhere on the campus or at other institutions. Such systems will frequently be specially designed to handle particular kinds of activity, and the microcomputer will be able to select the most appropriate one for the problem at hand.[18]

Administrative Computing:
Old Systems Versus New Systems

Diversity of Services and Complexity of Organization

Modern universities are among our most complex and difficult institutions to administer. Not only must they offer a wide range of courses at both undergraduate and graduate levels, but they also must provide housing and food, recreation, health care, counseling, and vocational placement services to the student. They must bill and collect tuition and other fees, offer financial aid arrangements, and maintain academic records. Moreover, laboratories and other facilities must be maintained and libraries operated and their collections continuously augmented and maintained. All these efforts and a variety of others must be financed through an aggressive garnering of funds from alumni, foundations, corporations, and government. All the while the entire organization must be administered and budgeted and new students and faculty recruited. At the same time, changes in the demand for instruction and research must be anticipated and accommodated. Smaller institutions are, of course, less complex than universities, but the number of courses offered is seldom small, a wide range of housekeeping and support services is required, and the need for planning and budgeting is similarly critical.

Organizational complexity and range of services in two institutions. Some sense of the diversity of services and complexity of administration in a large institution can be gained by an inspection of the directory of Columbia University, which provides a general picture of the organizational structure of that institution. The university is organized to carry out basic administrative support services such as accounting, payroll, personnel, purchasing, registration, bursar activities, facilities management as well as university development, computing services, university publications, public relations, development, grant administration, and a wide range of student services (e.g., disabled student services, residence halls, student activities, physical education).

An examination of the directory for Iona College, a much smaller institution (which limits its academic program to undergraduate studies and masters programs in business administration and computer science) indicates that although the organizational structure is much simpler and the range of services and functions requiring individual administrative offices much more restricted, there is, nevertheless, an extensive hierarchy of administrative machinery to provide for a broad array of services and administrative functions.

What such an analysis does not make clear, however, is, that a heavy administrative burden is borne by departments and schools; an extensive network of relationships and lines of communication must be maintained within and among departments, schools, and higher levels of administration; and administrators at all levels face a considerable burden when it comes to reporting for internal management and to meet the requirements of state and federal agencies and funding organizations.

Administrative responsibilities of departments and schools. Departments are the key operating organizations within the institution; they house the teaching and research faculties, carry out a variety of administrative tasks, and enjoy considerable powers of governance and policy determination. Departments initiate changes in curricula and new programs of study, recruit and recommend promotion of faculty and administrative staff (subject to the review of higher administration), advise students, schedule classes and the teaching hours of instructors, report grades, and administer academic programs for both undergraduates and higher degree candidates. Of equal importance, departments must control and plan their operations within the constraints of budgets that they initiate.

Schools are essentially small colleges and perform a number of major functions in addition to acting as administrative and planning headquarters for the departments under their jurisdiction. In virtually all schools such functions include admissions, student placement, external affairs and development, and financial aid. In some of the larger professional schools the range of functions may be quite broad indeed and may include student activities and the maintenance of separate computer facilities.

Extensive networks of relationships and lines of communication. The hierarchical structure and administrative range of universities and colleges make for an extensive network of communications and the need for information sharing. Moreover, there are anomalies in organizational structure that create even greater complexity. A few examples illustrate this point.

1. Admissions and registration require close coordination and the sharing of information, yet the two functions are typically separated. Admissions is carried out by schools, but registration is often the responsibility of the top-level administration.
2. The bursar's office is frequently separated organizationally from the office of the registrar, although both are involved in the registration process.
3. Personnel and payroll are typically separate offices, although both work continually with the individual records of employees.
4. A variety of functional offices require at least limited access to individual student records (e.g., departments, schools, student activities).

The burden of reporting. Reports must be prepared at all levels of administration for internal operations and to satisfy the requirements of government and funding organizations. The variety of such reports is enormous, and these reports cover matters ranging from academic performance, degrees granted, and financial aid to minority status of workers, utilization of research funds, completed maintenance activities, and parking permits.

What the foregoing makes clear is that the successful operation of universities and colleges involves coping with a heavy burden of recordkeeping, exchange of information, and reporting that in the face of rising costs, reduced funding, and adverse demographic trends challenges administrators to apply computer technology in new and more effective ways.

Administrative Computer Technology in Universities and Colleges

Universities were among the earliest users of computers, applying the new technology first to scientific research. As the technology became available for commercial applications, universities and colleges, like hospitals, governments, and larger business organizations, began to use computers for accounting, payroll, purchasing, and a variety of other recordkeeping applications. Early on, the computer center became the focus of computing activities, with data brought to the center for keypunching and batch processing and with programming and consulting services provided by center personnel. With time, keypunching has been largely replaced by batched data entry at terminals, frequently at the computer center but increasingly on line from offices around the campus. This still commonly used technology makes heavy use of paper records and files and has at best limited capability for on-line inquiry. Newest developments, however, use data-base technology that permits information to be captured at the source, combined with other related data, and held in computer memory. Information then is available on line (where appropriate) throughout the campus for inquiry and for downloading to the user's microcomputer for analysis and report preparation.

Administrative computing in the mid-1970s: A benchmark. No statistics are available on the extent to which universities and colleges utilize computers for administrative purposes today, either in terms of the range of applications or the degree to which modern new-era systems are employed. Information for the academic year 1976-1977 is available, however, which provides a useful benchmark.

This information is found in an inventory of computer usage in colleges and universities in which institutions were asked to indicate whether procedures for 109 functions in ten administrative categories (plus an eleventh, hospital applications) were carried out manually or were assisted by computers.[19] Table 4.3, compiled from the survey results, reveals that in the mid-1970s many institutions were making little use of computer technology and/or were using such technology only selectively. In only seven of the ten administrative categories did as many as 50 percent of the respondents report use of computers in any application (Table 4.4). In general, the most frequently reported applications of computers were those involving large volumes of data processing (class rosters, payroll), basic accounting procedures (general fund expenditures accounting), or major routine analysis and reporting (enrollment reporting, classroom utilization analysis).

Survey respondents were given the choice of indicating batch processing or on-line (the two were combined to indicate computer usage in Table 4.3 and 4.4), and in general, few (less than 10 percent) reported the latter. For this reason on-line computing responses were not analyzed. It is interesting to note, however, that in one category, library applications, on-line usage was reported as often or more often than batch processing in all applications but one (although the number of libraries reporting support in any application was less than 33 percent). We see here evidence of early efforts by libraries to use the technology in the manner described in the preceding discussion of academic computing.

No later surveys have been made that permit a similar analysis of institutional applications in the 1980s, but all information from the interviews and the literature indicated that an even greater disparity exists among universities and colleges today. Some institutions have

TABLE 4.3
Most Frequently Reported Computer Applications in Universities and Colleges,
1976-1977

Computer Applications[a]	Percentage
Admissions and records	
Class rosters	92
Term grade reporting	91
Term student records reports	90
Enrollment reporting	87
Enrollment statistics	86
Student registration process	85
Course add/drop processing	84
Student ethnic group reporting	78
Undergraduate admission process	73
Honors programs record	69
Course catalog records	66
Graduate admission processing	66
Schedule of classes preparation	65
Tuition and fee assessment	64
Student transcript records	64
High school testing records	59
Student class scheduling	58
General administrative services	
Facilities inventory	52
Classroom utilization analysis	51
Personnel records	50
Logistics and related services	
Equipment inventory	52

forged ahead by modernizing their systems and introducing a variety of new applications, while others have made little progress (although it is probably safe to say that virtually all have made some advances).

DAMIS: Columbia's blueprint of a modern system. A blueprint for development of a modern (although not state-of-the-art) administrative system has been accepted by one major institution as a target for implementation in the years immediately ahead. By examining briefly its major components and strategies we can gain an understanding of the principal characteristics of the new technology that are likely to be applied by other universities and colleges.

TABLE 4.3 cont.

Computer Applications[a]	Percentage
Financial management	
Payroll	87
General fund expenditures	74
Tuition and fee accounting	71
General fund ledger	68
Department expenditures	66
Resident hall accounting	59
General accounts receivable	59
Planning, management, institutional research	
HEGIS reporting	61
Budget position control	54
Faculty salary analysis	54
Budget analysis	51
Institutional cost studies	51
Auxiliary services	
Student directory	52
Office machine reporting control	51
Other administrative	
Test scoring and analysis	52

[a] Applications are shown for which 50 percent or more of institutions reported computer use.

Source: Compiled from J. W. Hamblin and T. B. Baird, *Fourth Inventory, Computers in Higher Education, 1976-1977* (Princeton, N.J.: EDUCOM, 1979), pp. xi-2, 3.

Such a planned system is the Distributed Administrative Management Information System (DAMIS) developed by Dr. Bruce Gilchrist and his colleagues at Columbia University. The proposed system (which was developed during a period of several years) represents a concrete plan for action. Several major elements are already in place.

In answering the question, "What is DAMIS?" the late Joseph Kroculick, one of the system's principal architects, stated:

DAMIS (Distributed Administrative Management Information System) is a systems architecture, the primary purpose of which is to provide

TABLE 4.4
Computer Use in Universities and Colleges, 1976-1977

Department	Number of Applications in Which	
	50% or More of Respondents Reported Computer Use	Less Than 50% of Respondents Reported Computer Use
Admissions, records	17	2
Financial management	7	21
Planning, management, institutional research	5	11
General administrative services	3	6
Auxiliary services	2	5
Logistics, related services	1	10
Other administrative	1	9
Financial aid administration	0	4
Physical plant operations	0	5
Library	0	8

Source: Compiled from J. W. Hamblin and T. B. Baird, *Fourth Inventory, Computers in Higher Education, 1976-1977* (Princeton, N.J.: EDUCOM, 1979), pp. XI-2, 3.

Columbia's schools and departments as well as the central administration with the means of obtaining and manipulating information required for the effective management and control of their functional areas.

DAMIS will be accomplished through a set of programs that will link departments and schools via terminals and communications lines directly to the University's central information data bases. DAMIS will allow the user to enter, track, change, extract and inquire data from the University data base and either, manipulate the data on the university's main computers or manipulate the data on the user's own micro computer or mini computer. This would be accomplished by providing the users with a single method to use their terminal or personal computers for the primary office functions of data entry and text processing.

DAMIS will allow the central database to be combined with the user's personal database and in some cases with other schools, departments or external data bases for the purpose of supplying needed information at the user's terminal or personal computer. DAMIS will allow the user to use his same terminal or personal computer for the primary office functions: data entry, data and text processing on personal computers (i.e., analysis and processing of text/data), data outputting (i.e., inquiry, reporting, transfer of data), data storage (i.e., storage of newly created data not otherwise stored on the University computers or user's personal computers).[20]

The background of the DAMIS effort is a significant clue to how modern systems evolve.[21] In 1979, Columbia began to replace several key systems with packaged (i.e., vendor-supplied) systems to cope with a number of problems that had developed. In the next few years, despite some benefits, much of the information provided by the new systems was neither timely nor accurate. Departments were making increasing use of their own manual data processing (and automated data processing in some cases), which led to a duplication of effort and generation of errors. A detailed study of two departments emphasized the importance of developing departmental information systems that would be integrated with the overall administrative system.

Since the early 1980s, task forces of computer specialists have worked with administrative officials and their staffs to plan new systems. An all university (including the medical school and Columbia Presbyterian Hospital) telecommunications system has been designed and largely put in place. Requirements and strategies for departmental information interconnections have been analyzed (but without implementation as yet), and a number of new systems have been implemented and old systems revised. Administrative systems within schools have been strengthened (especially in the Graduate School of Business where new hardware has been installed and new systems created).

Several aspects of Columbia's experience with the DAMIS plan may be applicable to other institutions. First, in order to meet its needs Columbia found it necessary to plan a system that would serve all branches and levels of the institution, including the departments, without duplication of recordkeeping or data entry. Second, such a system requires both integrated data-base architecture and major telecommunications networking capabilities. Third, the implementation of such a system requires major planning efforts and a great deal of money. Fourth, regardless of the human and financial resources that can be brought to bear on the total effort, implementation must proceed in a step-by-step fashion that at best takes a number of years.

Computerization in Four Institutions:
The Interviews

The four institutions interviewed for this study are discussed briefly below. A case history of one of these institutions, Stevens Institute of Technology, is presented in Appendix C. (Short case histories of the remaining institutions will be supplied by the author upon request.[22]) Two of the institutions interviewed are relatively small (Stevens Institute and Iona College), two quite large (Columbia University and New York University). The four differ not only in size and educational mission but also in the extent and manner in which computer and related technologies are currently being applied to teaching, research, and administration. They also differ in their strategies for implementing further applications of technology.

Stevens and Iona have both moved a considerable distance toward adopting modern technology (although in dissimilar ways) but have not encountered the problems of scale faced by Columbia and New York University (NYU). Columbia has moved somewhat further than NYU and is in the early stages of implementing major projects for a wide range of research, teaching, and administrative applications to its campuses. NYU has progressed unevenly. It has made major advances in computerization of library operations and offers a wide range of services at its academic computer facility but has not yet moved to bring new era computing to its administrative operations.

The Institutions Interviewed

Stevens Institute of Technology (Hoboken, N.J., enrollment of 3,000) was the first institution anywhere to require its students to purchase their own computers. CAI programs are used in calculus, chemistry, physics, engineering, and management. The campus is not networked, but Stevens is in the process of implementing a highly advanced telecommunications system. In the library, PCs are used for purchasing and tracking of orders and deliveries; cataloging is automated. Although administrative computing has not received as much attention as academic computing, student information, payroll, personnel, and accounting are modern systems.

Iona College (New Rochelle, N.Y., enrollment of 6,500) offers undergraduate and master's degrees in computer science and business administration. Computers play an important role in Iona's academic program, not only in computer science but in economics, psychology, physics, and business. In the library, Iona is moving agressively to computerize its operations and user services. Iona is quite advanced in administrative computing.

Columbia University (New York, N.Y., enrollment of 17,500) is in the process of overhauling its administrative systems to conform ultimately to its DAMIS blueprint. In academic computing, Columbia has made major advances in the library and in the Graduate School of Business, in addition to developing its scholarly Information Center. Its AURORA project provides a plan for bringing modern technology to teaching and research throughout the campus, but as yet academic computing has not made substantial progress in most of its schools and departments.

New York University (New York, N.Y., enrollment of 46,000) has proceeded unevenly in introducing modern technology. Its principal accomplishments thus far have been to establish its Academic Computing Facility and to move aggressively to computerize its libraries. NYU's major efforts in administrative computing have focused on financial operations that are still relatively labor- and paper-intensive and afford only limited on-line access. NYU has thus far been unsuccessful in putting into place a student information system and has as yet set forth no overall plan for making computer and related technologies available in support of research and teaching. It does, however, have a well-established computer science program, makes extensive use of computers in the sciences, and has brought computers into the administration of its schools of business.

The Outlook for Computerization
in the Years Just Ahead

The previous section briefly summarized the extent of computerization in four institutions of higher education. In the following discussion I draw upon the interviews and other evidence to assess the forces that are propelling U.S. universities and colleges toward further advances in the years immediately ahead and the obstacles that are likely to be faced.

Academic Computing

The role of the trailblazers. In recent years a number of institutions such as Dartmouth, Carnegie Mellon, MIT, the University of Houston, Stevens Institute of Technology, and Brown University have won recognition within the academic community for their achievements in applying computer technology across a broad range of courses involving all or most of their students. At the same time, individual schools of business and engineering (e.g., the Columbia Graduate School of Business and the Harvard Business School) are moving aggressively to bring computer support to their curricula. As these and others move rapidly forward, their progress is closely followed by many institutions that have yet to join the ranks of the vanguard.[23] The success of the front-runners establishes the feasibility of introducing computer applications to the classroom and provides critical information as to how best to implement new applications. This "demonstration effect" is strongly reinforced by educational journals such as the *Educational Chronicle* and conferences such as those sponsored by EDUCOM that familiarize officials and technical staff members with new programs and applications.[24]

The quiet revolution. The most significant advances, however, are not being made by the trailblazers but by libraries throughout the academic community that, as we have seen in each of the institutions interviewed, are computerizing their operations in order to cope with the explosive growth of publications. These libraries are working, frequently in league with computer service centers, to make available to students and faculty hundreds of on-line data bases. What is remarkable about these efforts is the extent to which they are supported by cooperative and private sector arrangements that permit participation by large and small institutions alike.

This is indeed a quiet revolution, for it has been little noticed by the press and is not well understood even on the campuses where it is occurring. Yet it represents an inexorable force propelling universities and colleges toward increasing their applications of technology in order to fulfill their academic missions.

Alternative paths to computer support. But these efforts do not necessarily lead directly to computer-aided instruction in the classroom or laboratory. They assist faculty and students in using the library, and where dial-in arrangements are available, they provide major resources to graduate students and faculty in carrying out research and in preparing papers. The full potential of these resources is realized, however, only when the campus is networked and microcomputers are widely accessible.

Institutions are faced with alternative paths to academic computer usage. They may proceed aggressively both to bring computers into the instructional program and to make library and on-line retrieval services available through networking and through making large numbers of microcomputers accessible or they may move passively and leave the initiative for utilizing computer-aided instruction to schools or individual departments. Just how rapidly institutions of higher education will move and what strategies they will adopt will depend on a number of factors including academic traditions, costs, leadership, and the alternatives for coping with the pressures of competition and rising costs.

Faculty resistance. Academic traditions are jealously guarded and not without reason. Colleges and universities are ancient institutions, and their methods of training students are time honored. On the other hand, computer-assisted education is new, and many of its applications are controversial. It is not surprising that faculties have been slow to experiment with computer technology.

Faculty resistance stems not only from skepticism grounded in tradition but from a clear recognition that application of technology to teaching and research involves a major commitment of time. For young teachers time spent preparing computerized materials is time deducted from research and publication, which are the basis for promotion and tenure.

For older faculty such an investment of time represents a postponement of cherished professional accomplishment and recognition.

Yet there is every reason to expect faculty resistance to aggressive computer applications in teaching and research to erode in time. Younger faculty members already are actively utilizing computers in research. They are comfortable with the new technology and aware of its potentials. For the most part, they may be expected to experiment with its use in teaching and to insist that their students use these resources in carrying out assignments and writing papers. As the new generation of teachers assumes a more important role in policy determination, there is reason to anticipate greater emphasis on computer-assisted instruction.

The need for funding. Clearly, a major obstacle to increased utilization of computers is cost. In time computer-assisted teaching may increase the ratio of students to faculty, at least for instruction in basic courses, and thus bring about economies. But for the years immediately ahead it is clear that computerization brings with it new demands for funding. Computing budgets that now account for roughly 3 percent, on average, of total expenditures may well rise to 6 percent.[25] Expenditures for mainframes will account for but a fraction. The installation cost of full-scale campus telecommunications networks may easily run into millions of dollars, and the cost of software and large banks of microcomputers is very large indeed. Somehow, in a period of rising operational costs and increasing competition for students, universities and colleges must find the funding for the new applications of technology. To the extent that these institutions are unable to do so the pace of computerization will be retarded.

Leadership. In the final analysis leadership appears to be the essential requirement for rapid progress toward utilization of computer technology. In every instance in which an institution has moved into the vanguard this appears to be true. The classic case of leadership at the top is generally recognized to be that of President John G. Kemeny at Dartmouth. But similar examples are to be found in the experiences of MIT, Stevens, and even the recent projects of Columbia. The failure of NYU to develop a more progressive effort would appear to be due to the fact that its leadership, however aggressive in other domains, has not yet addressed the issue of framing a program for computerizing either academic or administrative activities or of mounting any substantial effort to find the funds that make such an effort possible.

Alternative strategies for coping with competition. The administration of any institution has a variety of options open to it in coping with increasing competition and rising costs. It may move along traditional lines to bolster the institution's academic offerings; it may move more aggressively to enlist financial support from alumni and seek out new revenue sources; it may feature the increased application of technology to teaching and research to enhance the institution's appeal to undergraduates, graduate students, and potential new faculty; or it may move on more than one front. In the long run, however, university administrations cannot ignore the pressures from a new generation of students and faculty to support academic program more aggressively with the new tools of technology.

Administrative Computing

How are we to sum up the evidence regarding the probable course of future developments in administrative computing? At least four factors appear to restrict aggressive campuswide adoption of modern integrated data base systems.

The first is the highly dispersed nature of administrative and managerial work. The Columbia Directory (1984–1985) indicates that there are fifty-four departments and fourteen schools on the Morningside Campus (excluding the Faculty of Medicine and School of Oral and Dental Surgery), five major administrative offices under the president or executive vice presidents, twenty-four principal administrative areas under persons of vice presidential or similar rank, and more than ninety functional areas under directors or persons with titles indicating similar rank. If we simply regard each of these units as an administrative center where managerial and supporting clerical staff are grouped, we arrive at an estimate of more than 180 such centers. In all likelihood this is a very substantial underestimate because there are a variety of separate sub-centers unaccounted for, particularly within academic departments where a number of separate functions must be performed. Such an estimate is by no means inconsistent with the reported employment of 565 administrative and managerial personnel and 1,405 secretarial/clerical personnel on the Morningside campus. This crude calculation confirms that work takes place at many sites with few concentrations of personnel performing the same tasks. The implications for the application of computerization are important. It is not easy to build systems to improve administrative and managerial efficiency in such a fragmented and unstandardized environment.

A second factor is closely related to the first. Computerization is likely to proceed incrementally. Because it is difficult to build large systems that will effectively automate a wide variety of tasks, small systems are likely to be put into place. The task of subsequently combining these small systems with integrated systems must then be slow and fraught with difficulties.

A third factor restricting campuswide adoption, again closely related to the first two, is that existing organizational structures (evolved during the years out of earlier modes of carrying out work and assigning responsibility) often prevent a realization of efficiencies that should be forthcoming. In trying to learn about computing at Columbia University, the author spoke on several occasions with the late Joseph Kroculick, the information services official in charge of administrative computing, who contended that organizational structures posed the greatest obstacle to modernizing the university's administrative computer systems. Closely related functions were often overseen by different administrative heads with the result that consolidation of functions was impossible and coordination difficult. Similarly, the author was told by more than one New York University administrator that the failure thus far of the task force to bring about a modern student information system largely resulted from the inability of the various administrators to agree on what kind of system was needed or how the various units would participate.

A fourth restricting factor is the level of commitment to administrative computing. Although each of the institutions studied has moved to put into place major computerized administrative systems, nowhere was there a commitment equal to that being made to advance academic computing (with the possible exception of Columbia). Even at NYU far more has taken place to lay a foundation for future applications of technology in academic than in administrative computing. Additional evidence of this disparity between current efforts to strengthen academic and administrative systems can be found in a recent EDUCOM study of information processing planning activities on ten campuses that are aggressively engaged in computerization. In spite of lengthy treatment of strategies for enhancing academic computing, the reader finds only a few brief and casual references to administration.[26]

It seems likely that the explanation for this disparity lies, at least in part, in the fact that modern applications of technology to administration are not considered opportunities to reduce costs or to improve management. In none of the interviews was either possibility mentioned (although it was generally agreed that a heavier burden of activities could be accommodated through use of computerized systems without a matching increase in personnel). On several occasions administrators explained to the author that given the investment necessary, it was difficult to establish that computers actually had reduced the cost of operations, although there probably had been savings in earlier days when computer systems were first introduced. Just why cost savings were difficult to establish is not clear. One possible explanation lies in the fact that the burden of administrative work has increased at the same time that new technology has been applied. Another is that managers have not taken advantages of opportunities to cut costs by eliminating old work and reducing staff.

The issue of costs does not appear to have been systematically addressed in college and university administration. Cost accounting, as it is practiced in industry and as it is beginning to be practiced in hospitals under the new prospective payment arrangements, is virtually nonexistent in universities and colleges. Although both academic and administrative deans frequently operate under stringent budgets, there appears to be little or no effort to trace the sources of high costs. Even when facing financial difficulties, as NYU did during a period of near-bankruptcy in the 1970s and Columbia University during the early 1980s, efforts tend to be restricted to curtailing pay increases and additions to staff. In such an environment, computer systems are likely to evolve largely as means to address the increasing complexity of administrative tasks, while opportunities to reorganize administrative procedures and to reduce personnel and costs are neglected. The interview evidence seemed to indicate that such was the case. The author was not told of either significant reorganization or reduction in employment.

If this thesis is correct, administrative computing will face significant constraints in the years ahead. Yet, other factors will in all likelihood accelerate the pace at which the new technology replaces the old and enlarges the range of applications. One such factor may be that the progress of academic computing will encourage new efforts in administrative computing. This could occur for two reasons. The first is that institutions moving toward modern academic computing in a decentralized information processing environment must install campuswide telecommunications networks, and these will, in turn, create opportunities to integrate administrative systems because such facilities can be utilized jointly.

The importance of such networks seems well established. In the earlier EDUCOM study of campus computing strategies it was found that all ten campuses studied were actively investigating or had already installed experimental, high-capacity digital local area networks.[27] Similarly, among the four institutions interviewed here, two, Columbia and Iona, had campus networks in place. Stevens Institute had completed plans for a highly sophisticated $15 million system, and NYU, having already completed a new telephone system, was actively planning for a digital local area network.

The second reason is that the move toward installing modern academic computing facilities tends to be accompanied by a reorganization of institutional information processing staffs within a single administrative office in order to coordinate information processing activities. This was found to be true in eight of the ten progressive institutions studied by EDUCOM; one of the remaining two was actively considering the creation of such a position.[28] It was true also of Iona College and Columbia

University, where the most aggressive efforts to modernize administrative computing were being made.

Finally, one must not underemphasize the role of the demonstration effect, the cumulative effect of the steady improvement in technology, and the increasing availability of new and more versatile software. On balance, it seems safe to predict a steady, if not revolutionary, advance in the application of technology to administrative and managerial tasks in the years immediately ahead.

Computerization and Work

At least three conclusions relating to work and career opportunities can be drawn from the interviews and the limited employment data.

Academic and Administrative Computerization: The Dissimilar Implications for Employment

The first is that administrative, not academic, computerization is likely to have the principal impact on employment. To a considerable extent academic computing affects the way in which the student, undergraduate or graduate, acquires knowledge. This is not to say that the daily work— or even to some extent the required skills—of the teacher or researcher will not be altered. But technology is not likely to alter the process of recruiting new faculty members or of promoting them. No fundamental change in the way in which young scholars are being trained is apparent, although, of course, there is greater emphasis on the use of computers in graduate work, and graduate students are increasingly likely to be familiar with the use of computers in research. Moreover, the staff that supports academic computing is not large, involving principally the library and computer service center.

It is not inconceivable that in time academic computer and related technology may bring about fundamental structural changes in universities and colleges (e.g., academic instruction in the home, reorganization of schools and departments), but for the foreseeable future the employment impact of technology is likely to stem from changes in the way administrative tasks are performed, with clerical, secretarial, and managerial personnel affected most importantly.

The Impact of Computerization on Clerical and Secretarial Work

A second conclusion is that the content of clerical and secretarial work in universities and colleges is changing, albeit gradually, in ways quite similar to those observed in the New York City government and in hospitals. Where computer systems are replacing paper systems, filing and processing of paper forms are sharply reduced. One-time, on-line data entry and the ability to retrieve information on the screen of a terminal or microcomputer reduces the burden of very low-level clerical work and shifts work assignments to checking the accuracy of information, expediting the submission of data, or other tasks. At the lowest level, work is being destroyed, not added, but retraining makes it possible for existing personnel to perform new tasks and to respond to the increasing requests for information and reports. None of the interviewees indicated a marked increase in the difficulty of work, but in two of the institutions, managers asserted that they would be looking for personnel with greater ability to cope with system demands than had been recruited previously. In the other two institutions, managers appeared to be satisfied with past recruitment standards.

The conclusion to be drawn is that work is changing, but that recruitment standards are being modified only gradually and unevenly. But a hard, negative finding seems inescapable: Adoption of the new technology works in the direction of a more—not less—exacting screening of applicants. To the extent that this is true, fewer job opportunities are likely to open up in the relatively low-skilled occupations for those with only limited literacy and no familiarity with elementary computer applications.

The Declining Share of Clerical and Secretarial Jobs

A third conclusion strengthens the second. There has been a decline in the share of total university and college employment within the clerical/secretarial occupational category. Table 4.5 makes clear that in the interviewed institutions relatively few jobs were opened up in the ranks of secretarial/clerical personnel in any of the four institutions in recent years, while substantial growth occurred in administrative/managerial, professional nonfaculty, and technical/paraprofessional jobs in most or all of the four.[29] It also shows that for the United States as a whole during the 1979–1985 period, the relative performance of the several occupational groupings was similar. Secretarial/clerical employment showed the least change (declining slightly), and administrative/managerial, professional nonfaculty, and technical/paraprofessional employment increased significantly.

Although there is no direct evidence that the failure of clerical/secretarial employment to grow in step with total institutional employment is the result of computerization, the interview evidence strongly supported such a conclusion. All of the institutions studied grew in enrollment and, according to the interviews, faced new demands in

TABLE 4.5
Occupational Shares of Employment (1985) and Annualized Rates of Changes in Employment[a] in All U.S. Institutions of Higher Education and Four Interviewed Institutions[b]

	All U.S. Universities & Colleges	Stevens Institute of Technology	Iona College	Columbia University[c]	New York University
Faculty	29.2 (−.1)	26.4 (2.2)	42.8 (2.0)	21.9 (.1)	30.5 (.9)
Administrative managerial	10.0 (.8)	11.0 (−1.3)	26.1 (5.5)	12.8 (8.3)	17.9 (10.1)
Professional nonfaculty	14.8 (1.1)	8.7 (3.7)	.2 (0)	6.8 (12.2)	11.3 (2.4)
Technical/ paraprofessional	7.9 (.3)	5.1 (3.4)	4.1 (29.5)	6.3 (5.0)	
Secretarial/clerical	21.8 (−.2)	22.3 (1.0)	17.4 (4.6)	32.2 (1.4)	31.1 (.8)
Skilled crafts	3.3 (.1)	4.8 (−3.1)	3.1 (12.9)	4.6 (1.5)	3.3 (4.0)
Service maintenance	13.0 (−.5)	21.7 (1.9)	6.3 (21.4)	15.4 (.5)	5.9 (7.9)
Total	100.0 (.1)	100.0 (1.4)	100.0 (4.7)	100.0 (2.7)	100.0 (2.5)

[a] Occupational shares are shown first (without parentheses); annualized rates are shown second (within parentheses).
[b] Annualized rates are for the following periods: all universities and colleges, Iona College, and NYU, 1979–1985; Stevens Institute, 1977–1985; Columbia University, 1981–1985. In computing annualized rates of change the periods examined differ because of data availability. Employment data were available for all U.S. universities and colleges and for the four interviewed institutions for 1985, but comparable data were available for 1979 only for all universities and colleges, Iona, and NYU. For Stevens Institute, it was necessary to use 1977 for the beginning of the period; for Columbia, 1981.
[c] Excludes officers of research and officers of libraries.

Source: Data for four interviewed institutions were supplied by management. Data for all U.S. universities and colleges from Higher Education Staff Information Report (EEO-6) supplied by Equal Employment Opportunity Commission.

terms of information processed and reports rendered. All improved their administrative systems through computerization, although in different ways and to different degrees. Information on other institutions is sketchy, but such accounts as can be found in the literature indicated that advances in administrative computing have occurred generally.

Computerization and Managerial Work

It is intriguing that although managerial employment showed sharp increases in three of the four institutions and an above average increase in all U.S. institutions, the interviews indicated that few technological applications were as yet being made to managerial work. The increasing complexity of management and the increased emphasis on peripheral functions—not computerization—appear to be driving the demand for managers.

But there were a number of sophisticated applications being made of microcomputers (largely on a stand-alone basis), and these were assessed enthusiastically by users. Moreover, it is clear that wider use lies ahead. Joseph Kroculick of Columbia University pointed out that "managerial applications tend to come last." Only when modern systems are in place does the information for managerial planning and control become available. Given the organizational structure of universities and colleges, which is characterized by a relatively large number of administrative centers, there is good reason to expect a sharp rise in the use of microcomputers in budgeting, scheduling, planning, and related applications once microcomputers find their way into every office. Experience indicates that familiarity breeds not contempt but appreciation, and the logic of placing a microcomputer into the hands of every manager is to increase the level of sophistication of his or her performance.

Computerization and Other Work

Professors, managers, secretaries, and clerks account for roughly 60 percent of total employment in all U.S. institutions of higher education. The remainder is accounted for by professional nonfaculty (15 percent), technical/paraprofessionals (8 percent), skilled crafts (3 percent), and service/maintenance personnel (13 percent). Relatively little was learned from the interviews about the impact of computerization on these employees, but a few observations can be made.

The professional nonfaculty group includes a wide variety of professionals ranging from accountants, computer systems analysts, and researchers (nonteaching) to librarians, lawyers, public relations specialists, and vocational counselors. It is the most rapidly growing group for all U.S. institutions of higher education and for two of the three interviewed institutions for which data were available.[30] Similarly, the technical/ paraprofessional group includes a wide range of positions (for example, computer programmers, lab technicians, and draftspersons) and is growing at an above average rate in all institutions and quite rapidly in the three interviewed institutions for which data were available. The two groups are closely related in that both include technically specialized personnel; the distinction between them rests principally on levels of training, expertise, and credentials secured from formal training. Most of the personnel in both groups are involved in work that if not already affected by computerization, is likely to be affected within the near future.

Employment in the skilled crafts category is uniformly quite small; employment in the services/maintenance category is relatively large in all institutions and in two of the four interviewed institutions. According to the interviews, maintenance and repair work and, in general, work outside the areas of teaching, research, and office-type administration had been virtually untouched by applications of computer technology.

Computerization and Job Mobility

Perhaps the most important point regarding job mobility is that universities and colleges have never been characterized by extended career ladders. Assistant professors may, of course, rise to full professors, and some may be appointed to deanships if they demonstrate administrative capacity and an inclination for such work. But the opportunities for advancement among low-level clerical, secretarial, and maintenance personnel are seldom favorable. Some may rise to middle-level administrative posts within the department or division in which they work, but most middle- and upper-level administrators are likely to be professionals hired from outside the institution.[31] Complex administrative structures and a tradition of autonomy also limit opportunities for advancement. Personnel do not move readily from one administrative unit to another; typically, they must look for promotional opportunities within their own units.

In recent years some efforts have been made to provide better opportunities for advancement, particularly for women. Able secretaries with college degrees have advanced to positions of assistant dean, assistant director, or even director. In some instances, such as Student Information Services at Columbia, there has been a restructuring to create some new, better paying, and more responsible positions.

At the same time, the increasing importance of professional nonfaculty and technical/paraprofessional personnel is creating a new type of compartmentalization, for these jobs are open only to those properly qualified—graduates of technical schools, colleges, and universities or from other organizations. Thus far these developments appear to be largely unrelated to computerization. But to the extent that applications of technology to administrative systems do restrict the employment opportunities for those without college or technical training, the future is likely to bring a reduction of opportunities for employment and career mobility.

Notes

1. V. W. Plisko and J. D. Stern, *The Condition of Education* (Washington, D.C.: National Center for Educational Statistics, 1985 edition), p. 88.

2. Ibid., p. 88.

3. Ibid., p. 114.

4. E. R. Fiske, "Colleges' Tuition up 7-8%, Total Bill Can Exceed $16,000", *New York Times*, April 7, 1986, p. 1.

5. E. R. Fiske, "Colleges Facing Age Shift Find Small Is Better," *New York Times*, March 10, 1986, p. 1.

6. J. Francis Rientzes, "New Technology for Storing, Retrieving and Disseminating the Professional Literature," in D. Mebane, ed., *Solving College and University Problems through Technology* (Princeton, N.J.: EDUCOM, 1981), p. 397.

7. John M. Haar, "The Politics of Information: Libraries and Online Retrieval Systems," *Library Journal*, February 1986, p. 40.

8. Access to these other other data bases is most commonly acquired by libraries but could be arranged through computer centers or by an individual department.

9. Carol Tenoper, "Database Directories: In Print and Now On Line," *Library Journal*, August 1985, p. 64, and John M. Haar, "The Politics of Information: Libraries and Online Retrieval Systems," *Library Journal*, February 1986, p. 40.

10. During the academic year 1982–1983 Columbia University Libraries supplied 16,476 volumes and photocopies. *Columbia Libraries Annual Report 1982-1983*, p. 7.

11. Faculty members or graduate students who own personal computers may in many institutions dial in from their homes.

12. This description of the workstation is based on William Crossgrove and Roger Henkle, "Networks of Scholars' Workstations/Appropriate Technology for Brown University," April 18, 1983, unpublished.

13. Greg Kearsley, "Embedded Training: The New Look of Computer-Based Instruction," in Mebane, *Solving College and University Problems*.

14. Derek Bok, *The President's Report 1983–84* (Boston, Mass.: Harvard University, 1984), p. 2.

15. Ibid.

16. Crossgrove, "Networks of Scholars' Workstations," p. 4.

17. Ibid.

18. From the appendix in N. N. Mintz, P. M. Battin, and B. Gilchrist, "Project Aurora. A Columbia University Education Project," Columbia University, November 1984, unpublished.

19. J. W. Hamblin and T. B. Baird, *Fourth Inventory, Computers in Higher Education, 1976–1977* (Princeton, N.J.: EDUCOM, 1979), pp. xi–02. Respondents were asked to indicate the manner in which a function was being performed: (1) manual; (2) bookkeeping machine; (3) ledger accounting; (4) EAM only; (5) computer: batch processing; (6) computer: on line. In Table 4.3 numbers 5 and 6 are combined. The number of institutions reporting numbers 2, 3, 4 was negligible and the number reporting number 6 was in most instances small (much less than 10 percent). The reader should note that response rate to this question on the survey was poor. No more than 1,052 of the 3,136 institutions responding to other parts of the questionnaire indicated practice for any given application. The editors of the survey caution that many institutions apparently felt that where computers were not in use it was unnecessary to answer the question. Accordingly, it would appear that the number of institutions not making use of computers (i.e. using type 1–4 methods) is underestimated.

20. J. Kroculick, "Distributed Administrative Management Information System (DAMIS)", Columbia University, April 2, 1985, unpublished, p. 2.

21. R. Juckiewicz and J. Kroculick, "Distributed Administrative Management Information System (DAMIS)," Proceedings of the 1983 CAUSE National Conference, "Information Resources and the Individual," December 11–14, 1983, pp. 1–2.

22. Address requests to T. M. Stanback, Jr., Conservation of Human Resources, Columbia University, 2880 Broadway, N.Y., N.Y. 10025.

23. Officials of Stevens Institute of Technology stated that they had been visited by representatives of more than 200 institutions who wished to observe their program firsthand.

24. EDUCOM is a nonprofit consortium of more than 500 colleges and universities interested in sharing information technology resources, cooperative efforts, and technology transfer. EDUCOM's principal focus is academic applications of technology. CAUSE is a similar organization that focuses on administrative applications.

25. The average computer facility budget was 2.7 percent of the institution's budget in 1984–1985, up from 2.1 percent in 1980–1981. See Charles W. Warlick, ed., *1985 Directory of Computing Facilities in Higher Education* (Austin: University of Texas at Austin Computation Center, undated), p. A-7. The estimate of 6 percent was provided by Edward A. Friedman of Stevens Institute of Technology in an interview. Dr. Friedman also has stated that even a relatively unambitious program for undergraduate engineering students may be expected to involve expenditures equaling about 5 percent of the total cost of four-year engineering education. See E. A. Friedman, "The Wired University," *IEEE Spectrum*, November 1984, p. 119.

26. John W. McCredie, ed., *Campus Computing Strategies* (Princeton, N.J.: EDUCOM, 1983).

27. Ibid., p. 14.

28. Ibid.

29. It is not clear why employment data for Stevens Institute of Technology showed a decline in the managers/administrators category. Interviewees were unaware of such a change but did note that there had been a substantial reorganization of the administrative structure during the period. It is also not clear why there was no employment change in the professional nonfaculty classification at Iona, when employment grew extremely rapidly in the technical professional category (almost quadrupling during the period 1979–1985). One possible explanation is that some work was reclassified from the higher to the lower level of specialization.

30. At NYU there was evidence that definitions of professional nonfaculty personnel and technical paraprofessionals may have changed in the reporting of 1985 data, so the two were combined in Table 4.5. The data supplied indicated that professional nonfaculty employment did increase substantially, however.

31. For example, at NYU the chiefs of payroll accounting, budget accounting, and accounts payable and the assistant registrar had risen from low-level clerical posts. The controller, however, was a professional accountant hired from the outside. Similar examples could be cited for the other institutions.

5

Future Directions

In the beginning of this study, I pointed out that the major types of nonprofit institutions to be analyzed—government (as represented by the City of New York), hospitals, and universities and colleges—shared certain characteristics. They are large service organizations producing a variety of unstandardized products with, traditionally, little assistance from labor-saving technology; they are complex organizations made up of a number of loosely knit departments or agencies with relatively weak top-down control and lax, unsophisticated approaches to cost accounting and control; and, finally, they are institutions currently under pressure to bring about closer cost control, tighter organization, and more informed planning.

The interview material and other evidence have made clear that these are indeed shared characteristics. The evidence has shown also that each institution is engaged in a process of applying the new computer technology to a variety of activities and that this new technology, along with certain organizational and institutional changes that are being wrought, is altering the way in which work is done and services are produced.

The Issue of Productivity Gains
in Nonprofit Organizations

The implications of these findings are that the major nonprofit organizations, although all under duress, face important opportunities for cost control and revitalization. This view, however, is not commonly held. In general, nonprofit organizations and, indeed, a wide range of other services, have been considered low productivity activities that are not only less efficient than goods-producing activities but are unlikely to show substantial improvement in the years ahead. In the view of many, the rise of services and nonprofit services in particular is largely responsible for what is generally held to be a slowdown in productivity in the U.S. economy in recent years.

The Baumol Model

The clearest theoretical statement supporting this view was the analysis of William Baumol, which was first presented in a much quoted article in the *American Economic Review* almost two decades ago.[1] We would do well to examine his arguments and to observe the extent to which his model is or is not applicable to nonprofit organizations as they have been observed in this study.

Baumol's basic premise was "that economic activities can . . . . be grouped into two types: technologically progressive activities in which innovations, capital accumulation, and economies of large scale all make for a cumulative use in output per man hour and activities which, by their very nature, permit only sporadic increases in productivity."[2] In the former, he holds, "labor is primarily an instrument, an incidental requisite for the final product"; in the latter (which included municipal government, hospitals, colleges, and universities), "the labor is for all practical purposes the end product itself."[3]

His argument stripped to its essentials is that in a world in which the former class of activities is experiencing more or less continual increases in productivity, labor will press for and receive in higher wages its share of the increasing output and thereby induce similar rates of increase in wages in the latter unproductive sector. Thus, "If productivity per man rises cumulatively in one sector relative to its rate of growth elsewhere in the economy, while wages rise commensurately in all areas, then relative costs (and prices) in the nonprogressive sectors must inevitably rise."[4]

The adjustment process that follows, he argued, depends upon the elasticity of demand. If elasticity is low, higher prices will be paid, and effective demand undergoes little change. If elasticity is high, effective demand will shrink and the activity will be driven from the marketplace or patronized only by a select few. The demand for medical services and higher education are essentially inelastic, but the demand for services of municipal government is susceptible to continual deterioration as a result of rising costs and higher taxes.

In the case of large municipal government, the adjustment process is exacerbated by the presence of unfavorable externalities related to size. Larger populations increase the cost of services disproportionately (doubling traffic more than doubles congestion costs, and pollution rises geometrically not proportionately as population increases). Thus, complexity and rising costs per unit of services drive the city toward cumulative decay as businesses and middle-class residents seek alternative locations as the tax base erodes and as underfunded maintenance causes capital infrastructure to deteriorate.

There is abundant evidence that historically costs have risen disproportionately in each of the nonprofit institutions studied here and that each has faced or is facing a crisis that is at least in part due to the high cost of operations. Yet how applicable is this model in assessing the outlook for the years ahead? Does the introduction of the new technology along with associated changes in organization and management offer significant opportunities for stemming or reversing the trend toward rising costs, or are these but palliatives in a sector in which fundamental economic factors dictate inevitable increases in costs?

In answering this question three observations seem relevant. The first, which questions a basic premise of Baumol's model, is that labor itself is not the end product in nonprofit institutions.[5] Equating labor with the service rendered is perhaps a reasonable simplification in certain service activities, such as a string quartet or a dance troupe, where productivity cannot be increased save, perhaps, in certain restricted administrative functions and a rise in wages must bring a roughly proportionate increase in total cost and price of the final service produced.

But it is not true in city government, in hospitals, or in universities and colleges. All these institutions, as we have seen, are complex, multifunction organizations in which work can be rearranged, organizational structures changed, and costs reduced. Treating the patient is not simply carried out by the physician and the nurse; educating the student, by the teacher alone; or the rendering of city services by the police, firefighter, or sanitation worker. New arrangements are possible for the rendering of services and for the provision of the elaborate but necessary administrative support services. In short, in the language of the economist, the production function can be altered to bring about economies in the nonprofit services just as it is continually being altered in manufacturing and other nonservice activities.

Second, the new computer technology is multidimensional in its impact. At one level modern computer systems abridge labor in ways analogous to modern equipment in the plant, thereby reducing the time required to do a task and eliminating some tasks entirely. But these systems, at another level, create opportunities and even necessitate, changed organizational arrangements. Because old administrative structures were at least in part the reflection of old modes of carrying out work, new structures may be required to accommodate a new technology in which information is shared and new managerial opportunities and responsibilities are opened up at all levels of the organization.

Further, and at a still different level, the new technology brings opportunities to change the product itself. In city government, we see, for example, how the inspection of buildings is simplified and improved and the information accumulated is made instantly available to firefighters, how citizen housing complaints can be registered more quickly and dealt with more effectively, how snow removal equipment can be scheduled more efficiently. In hospitals, we observe how systems can accelerate scheduling and reporting of procedures, and laboratory, radiology, and pharmacy professionals can instantly gain access to patient and technical information in order to more effectively execute their duties. In universities, we observe how the researcher and student can be provided with additional data sources and the teacher with new instructional aids.

Third, the adjustment process is more complex than that envisaged by Baumol. It does not take place simply through demand-side changes—the effect of price on effective demand. It also involves a supply-side process in which functions involved in production are altered and work and organizational structure may be changed.

In short, the burden of evidence of this study indicates that the scope for change and for increases in productivity is far wider than that envisaged in the earlier theory. Nonprofit organizations are not locked into modes of operation that must result in relentlessly rising costs.

An Alternative Model of Development

Thus, the evidence suggests a very different model in which nonprofit organizations, driven by two sets of forces, bring about modes of service delivery and organizational arrangements that result in leaner staffs, rising productivity, and an altered range of services. The first set of factors is clearly the new technology. Here, the nonprofit sector, whose basic modes of production have been largely untouched by earlier technological revolutions, is involved for the first time in a true industrial revolution—one that radically alters production functions to increase productivity.[6] This technology affects virtually every phase of operations either directly or indirectly and brings substantive opportunities for managerial planning and control and for the reorganization of work.

The second set of forces comprises increasing competition and other pressures for reduction of costs and improvement of services and, accordingly, the adoption of the new technology. Nonprofit organizations have in the past been largely insulated from the need to increase efficiency by the absence of competition, by burgeoning demand, by access to governmental subsidies, and, in the case of hospitals, by favorable arrangements of third-party payment. Now the tide has turned.

Each of the nonprofit institutions studied herein is facing the challenge of operating in an environment that now requires sharp improvements in productivity. Hospitals and universities and colleges face increased interinstitutional competition, new institutional arrangements, and reductions in funding from government and other sources. Municipal governments encounter widespread demands for tax reductions, funding reductions, and rising needs for service delivery.

Given the broad applicability of the technology and the strength of the pressures for change, the developmental process, in time, should bring about significant modifications in these institutions. In each we are likely to see virtually across-the-board applications of technology to administration and to delivery of services accompanied by major changes in organizational structures and, perhaps most important, improvements in management's ability to control operations and to plan.

It seems likely that such changes also will contribute significantly to a revision of the missions of nonprofit organizations and some change in their relations with private sector institutions. In city government there should be a greater scope for experimentation with alternative arrangements for service delivery, especially as regards increased utilization of private sector agencies to perform certain functions. Thus far efforts to "privatize" have been hampered by an inability of city government managers to compare costs of government in-house operations and private sector providers and by an inability to properly monitor the latter. The new technology opens up opportunities for cost accounting in the nonprofit sector (as witnessed in DRG accounting in some hospitals) and for monitoring and tying-in with contracting firms (as witnessed in the cases of streetlight maintenance in New York City and in purchasing arrangements between American Hospital Supply Company and its customers).

Among hospitals the new technology should go far to facilitate the major institutional changes that are already under way and to bring about a rationalization of the roles played by each type of institution. With better knowledge of costs as well as closer control of operations, management will be better positioned to determine which services are appropriately delivered by the hospital and which are best left to alternative arrangements. At the same time, the technology should facilitate the integration of hospitals into larger health care systems where such integration is appropriate.

The role of this technology in higher education is more difficult to assess but may ultimately be more decisive. Universities and colleges with their high costs and high fees would appear to be vulnerable to innovative competition. Although these institutions for generations have been centers for liberal arts, undergraduate education, research, and the training of scholars, they have increasingly been called upon to act as training institutions for the marketplace and as credentialers of those young people who seek careers with opportunities for advancement. The task of continuing to perform traditional roles while providing suitable training for the career needs of students young and old and doing so at costs competitive with those of institutions with more limited objectives is a formidable one. It seems likely that in the years ahead there will be considerable reexamination of the roles of the various institutions and some sorting out of functions of undergraduate, graduate, and adult education and research within an environment of vigorous competition and innovation. Under such conditions technology, especially as applied to teaching, is likely to play a major role.

Implementing Adoption of the New Technology

For many individual organizations the outlook is problematic. How well each succeeds in overcoming its difficulties depends in considerable measure on its ability to implement the new technology and to institute improved modes of operation. Several findings from the interviews and other evidence shed light on the prospects for implementing adoption of the new technology.

The Incremental Nature of Implementation

Adoption of computerization takes place incrementally. Large, integrated systems are unlikely to be put in place in a single effort. Rather, implementation typically takes place by building separate systems (e.g., tax appraisal and legal tracking systems in the city, patient care and billing systems in the hospital, alumni information and registration systems in universities and colleges) that may be subsequently linked.

But the opportunities for step-by-step implementation extend far beyond the successive building of major component systems. The new technology can be introduced in a multitude of ways, several of which have been described in the earlier chapters. A variety of small subsystems, such as pharmacy systems, DRG analysis systems, simple admissions and discharge systems, can be brought in on a stand-alone basis through the use of microcomputers. Moreover, microcomputers can be utilized in virtually every workplace for word processing or other special stand-alone requirements. Applications can be added as desired and can be linked ultimately to systems of larger and larger scope.

The rapidly increasing popularity of the versatile microcomputer deserves special emphasis in any consideration of the implementation of the new computer technology. Although no data on installations in

TABLE 5.1
Total Annual Microcomputer Shipments, 1981–1986 (in thousands of units)

Year	Shipments
1981	900,000
1982	2,600,000
1983	6,100,000
1984	7,800,000
1985	7,700,000
1986 (projected)	7,900,000

Source: Estimated from graph of annual shipments of personal computers costing less than $10,000. John W. Wilson, "Computers: When Will the Slump End?" *Business Week*, April 21, 1986, p. 61.

nonprofit organizations are available, some sense of the increase in usage throughout the U.S. economy can be gained from statistics for total annual shipments of microcomputers since 1981 (see Table 5.1).

Given the rapid price decline of microcomputers, the very large numbers of software programs now available in the market, and the continual improvement in microcomputer capability and range of applications, it is clear that we are rapidly moving into an era in which the personal computer will become virtually ubiquitous. Its ready availability will in the years ahead do much to facilitate the building of larger systems.

Problems of Selecting Equipment and Software

A major obstacle to implementation is the difficulty of selecting appropriate hardware and software in building systems that meet the special needs of individual organizations. The number of vendors, particularly for peripheral equipment and software, is large, and the products offered vary widely in terms of price and design. Moreover, the flow of work and, frequently, organizational structure will require alteration to accommodate both the operational characteristics of the hardware and the limitations imposed by software programming.

The interviews offered abundant testimony to the seriousness of these problems. Most of the institutions had at one time or another found it necessary to call in consultants, and all reported lengthy delays in arriving at decisions on appropriate hardware. In some instances, such as the search for a student records system at NYU and attempts by several of the libraries to locate subsystems that would meet their needs, efforts were unsuccessful. In other instances, systems were adopted but later proved to be inadequate (e.g., the Columbia University experience in the early 1980s). One hospital manager reported wistfully, "We've gone through, literally, many packing boxes of specifications in search of the right hardware."

A major problem in putting a new system into place is the incompatibility of the hardware and software of different vendors. Very recently, major efforts have been made by leading vendors to bring about standardization, and both peripheral equipment manufacturers and software producers are struggling to achieve some compatibility, but the problem remains a major one.

Moreover, new problems of implementation are being created by the movement toward networking. John W. Wilson, in a *Business Week* article, examined the recent slowdown in computer industry revenues and found

> a wrenching transition that is changing the way computers are sold, lengthening the buying process and creating new organizational and even psychological problems for the people who use them. The catalyst for all this is a move away from simple number crunching toward information networks. These networks ease the communication of data and put more reliance on small and medium-sized machines than on the giant mainframes that dominated computer strategies of the past.[7]

He further noted that in taking advantage of the economies of smaller computers users "must tie together a vast array of often incompatible gear, find software that can operate on many different machines, and develop new strategies for storing and securing information and routing it around their companies."[8]

Finally, the possibility of building systems by step-by-step additions of hardware and software both facilitates and complicates the task of modernization. On the one hand, such additions make it possible for the institution to move forward within the constraints of available funds and the ability of management and staff to accommodate change. However, on the other, these additions create new problems when the freestanding subsystems have to be stitched together later on. In the end, the building process may stop before a fully effective total system is put in place or the final larger system may function suboptimally.

Financial Constraints

In the previous chapters I have noted repeatedly that modern computer systems are expensive to buy and to operate. If the estimates for universities and colleges are anywhere near the mark for hospitals and municipal governments, current computer-telecommunications budgets will need to increase by a factor of at least two and probably more.

Yet, funding is likely to prove more difficult than in the past. Among hospitals, there is little chance that generous third-party-payer arrangements for reimbursement of capital expenditures that were obtained in the past will be continued in the years ahead. Among universities and colleges, the very substantial support provided by major vendors in order to encourage early adoption of academic systems can hardly be expected to continue once virtually all institutions are involved. Similarly, the budget provisions in New York City government that favored expenditures for major systems over personnel expenditures in order to implement the new programs for reorganization and increased productivity are not likely to be sustained.

Thus, there are major questions regarding the funding of a widespread effort to bring modern computer systems to nonprofit organizations throughout the economy. It seems likely that future arrangements will involve leasing or some other type of for-profit/nonprofit institutional cooperation and that funding will in some degree act to slow down the pace of computerization.

Problems of Organizational Rigidities and Leadership

For many of these institutions, organizational rigidities and lack of leadership are likely to prove the principal obstacles to an expeditious introduction of more advanced systems. The semiautonomous nature of individual departments in municipal government and hospitals and of schools and academic departments in universities and colleges has tended to weaken the hand of top management and has strengthened the tendencies for lower organizations to develop independent and frequently conflicting operational objectives. In cities, political objectives, rather than operational efficiency, are likely to receive high priority. In hospitals and institutions of higher education, a preference for traditional approaches to health care delivery, teaching, and research is likely to generate resistance to the diversion of financial or human resources in order to facilitate computer systems and their associated organizational changes.

Under these conditions top management will often face formidable obstacles in effecting major changes. Only where leaders are successful in making it clear that this technology can increase competitiveness, improve the quality of service, and reduce or constrain costs, is implementation likely to proceed rapidly. Where such success does not occur, advances are likely to be made with difficulty.

Forces Propelling Adoption

At the same time that these largely negative factors are acting to constrain adoption, there are at least three major countervailing forces: the demonstration effect, the rise of a younger generation adept in and enthusiastic about working with the technology, and advances in the technology itself.

New technology is by its nature unfamiliar. Its adoption poses problems of adjustment and in the early, awkward stages may fail to bring about hoped for results. As more and more organizations adopt the technology, as problems of implementation are solved, and as the potentials for increasing efficiency and lowering costs are demonstrated, the task of introduction becomes easier, and the advantages become more evident. The technology is accepted, and the pace of adoption accelerates.

Similarly, acceptance grows as more and more individuals who are familiar with the technology and are at ease with it become a part of the organization. This "changing of the guard" is an incremental process but a cumulative one as well. Younger personnel and some of the older generation increasingly are being trained in the use of computers or are gaining familiarity through ownership of personal computers. With each passing year, their ranks swell within all organizations, both nonprofit and profitmaking, and as these staff members move to positions of greater responsibility, they play a greater role in determining policy.

Finally, the rapid advance of technology makes its application increasingly attractive. The introduction of powerful minicomputers and microcomputers at steadily declining prices and the dramatic improvement in computing power bring the technology within the reach of an ever-larger number of organizations. At the same time, rapid improvements in systems design and the increased availability of powerful and highly applicable software make new systems more effective. Similarly, new peripheral equipment, especially the development of telecommunications, video disk, and massive memory storage technology, increases the range of possible applications.

Outlook for the Decade Ahead

Although the constraints and opportunities sketched in this study will work together to determine the pace at which nonprofit organizations adopt the new technology in the years ahead, whatever occurs must take place against a base-line of the systems, old or new, that are in use today. The interviews and such data as are available indicated that there is a wide variation in practice, both within and among organizations, and that, on balance, the movement toward modern systems is still in an early stage. At the same time, we find that all organizations are involved in planning for and putting into place such systems.

The years just ahead will see these plans completed and others formulated and achieved, but it is likely that the installation of tele-communications systems and the linking of existing systems will in many instances act to constrain the rate of advance. In short, new applications will continue at a more or less steady rate, with some institutions well in the lead of others. It seems unlikely that another half-decade will bring a full conversion to the technology discussed in this study.

But the changes, nevertheless, will be cumulative. The coming five years should see a marked change in the extent to which on-line integrated systems are being utilized and a significant increase in utilization of distributed processing arrangements.

It seems likely that the most dramatic change will be in the use of microcomputers. Several factors should contribute to this growth.

1. Economy: Microcomputers are cheap enough to be purchased out of departmental budgets without regard to overall capital expansion plans.
2. Versatility: Microcomputers can be used for a wide variety of applications in either stand-alone or network mode.
3. Growing familiarity: A rapidly increasing number of employees at all levels are becoming familiar with the use of PCs.
4. Application to managerial tasks: Finally, because the use of microcomputers for lower- and middle-managerial tasks is as yet in its infancy, a rapid increase in such application would appear a virtual certainty.

If this scenario for the five years just ahead is roughly correct, the following half-decade should see rapid movement toward widespread adoption of large integrated systems. Networks should by then be largely in place, and organizational changes will have been at least partially effected, so that the logic and advantages of the new systems will be generally appreciated. Several college generations trained in the use of computers will have entered the work force, and a very large number of high school graduates with at least basic computer skills will have been employed. Institutional resistance to the technology by then should have largely subsided.

Such forecasts as the above are, of course, only educated guesses. Some information pertaining to probable developments is well estab-lished; some is not. Perhaps the greatest issue is the extent to which these institutions will consider themselves at risk. It is quite clear that the major computerization efforts made by the City of New York stemmed from the crisis of the mid–1970s and those of hospitals from the pressures of employers and third-party payers to reduce costs, from growing competition, from reduced government support, and from the new prospective payment arrangements. Universities and colleges also have faced major problems of declining enrollments, increased competition, and the need to raise tuition, but have as yet moved less forcefully to adopt technology as a strategy for survival.

It is possible that future events will bring some reduction in this sense of urgency. A period of prosperity and/or political developments that bring more generous federal funding might well reduce the pressure on these institutions to effect the changes needed to deliver services with leaner and more efficient staffs. But each of these nonprofit organizations is vulnerable, and more likely than not, the difficulties of each will mount rather than diminish. For cities, the problem of providing for the needs of minorities shows no signs of abating, and the competition with suburbs and outlying areas for firms and middle-class residents continues. For hospitals, increases in the cost of health services have yet to be brought under control, and the trend toward new and competitive institutional arrangements suggests a future downsizing of these institutions and a reduction of their role to the provision of acute patient care.

The situation facing universities and colleges is more ambiguous. At the same time that the demographic cohort from which college students have traditionally been drawn is declining, the importance of postsecondary education is increasing. Perhaps of greater importance is the growing potential for more damaging competition than has thus far been faced. The threat of increasing competition arises because of the very high levels of college tuitions and fees. Today, annual charges in private institutions may be more than $10,000 and for some as much as $14–$16,000. Thus far, these institutions have sought to cope with the difficulty of recruiting students by arranging for student loans and, more recently, by instituting new arrangements by which parents may finance their children's education by prepayment during the years prior to college. But such arrangements are poor substitutes for lower charges, and as we have seen, students are turning to less expensive state-supported institutions.

The potential for competition extends well beyond state-supported institutions, however. A very large amount of formal training is already being carried out by employers through in-house programs, seminars, and institutes. But perhaps of greater significance is the rapid increase in the number of degree-granting institutions established by corporations (e.g., General Motors, Northrop Aircraft, McDonald's Corporation), industrywide associations (e.g., Institute of Textile Technology, the College of Insurance, American Graduate School of International Management), and professional, research, and consulting associations (e.g., Arthur D. Little Management Education Institute, the Rand Corporation's Graduate Institute, the American Management Association's Institute of the Midwest Industrial Management Association).

In a study prepared for the Carnegie Institute for the Advancement of Teaching and published in 1985, Nell P. Eurich identified and studied eighteen such institutions with multiple degree programs.[9] In addition, she learned that five corporations plan to start at least nine more degree-granting programs in the "near future" and that "by 1988, eight corporations propose to offer about twenty more college-level programs."[10]

Although some of these institutions operate as an integral part of the sponsoring corporation, others are independent nonprofit institutions. All are directly or indirectly in competition with more traditional institutions and offer a number of major challenges. Dr. Eurich reported a growing use of technology in support of teaching (e.g., videocassettes, microcomputers, and other technological aids). She also reported that highly flexible arrangements are offered for pursuing continued postgraduate training, and, in at least one institution, provisions are made for study without residency requirements. Finally, she observed that "corporate education challenges higher education to clarify and reaffirm its mission. . . . Because the corporate classroom is ultimately concerned about productivity and performance, its goals are apt to be specific, even narrow. Such non- traditional education has an essential place in our society. And established colleges and universities may learn from its processes and procedures."[11]

Thus, universities and colleges, like hospitals, face the prospect of operating in a competitive environment that demands cost reductions and new approaches to rendering services. Because the modern systems offer promise of assistance on both counts, it seems likely that the years ahead will see increasingly aggressive efforts to utilize computers for both academic and administrative purposes.

Computerization and Employment

Changes in Work

In assessing the impact of modern computer systems on work, it is useful to observe three distinguishing characteristics: first, the ability of the user to enter, store, and retrieve vast amounts of information in these data-base systems; second, the ability of the user to communicate with and transfer information to the main computer or other computers and other workplaces; and third, the ability of the user to carry out sophisticated, complex manipulations of data and to store the results in memory where desired. Together these basic capabilities of the technology make possible a vast array of applications that affect work in a number of fundamental ways.

1. They make it possible to eliminate repetitious paperwork involving entering and filing information and to eliminate time-consuming, repetitious calculations.
2. They eliminate or simplify a number of difficult and complex operations including scheduling, monitoring, and tracking in order to facilitate control of operations.
3. They provide instant access to information stored as a result of previous operations or to specialized data bases of technical information.
4. They make it possible to share information throughout the organization without moving files or interrupting the work of others and to utilize such information for a variety of administrative, planning, and control functions as well as for the preparation of routine or specialized reports.

Taken together, these applications affect clerical, administrative, and managerial work at all levels as well as the work of a variety of technicians and professionals. At the lowest (largely clerical) levels, much routine work is eliminated, but new work is created. Opportunities are opened up to deal directly with clients or vendors, and a larger amount of information is likely to be collected and dealt with in the process of carrying out daily operations. Work tends to center on the computer terminal, and because all processing is simplified by the computer (e.g., the computer prompts, provides necessary reference information, etc.), the scope of the assignment is likely to be broadened, or even where work is confined to original data entry, the volume of work for which the operator is responsible is increased. In general, more is expected of the worker in terms of familiarity with the overall functioning of the operation and of his or her ability to cope with problems that arise.

At higher levels there again are opportunities to eliminate tedious work; at the same time, new work is generated, and new information must be assimilated. Professionals and technicians are beginning to find relief from onerous chores, and in some instances they are able to consult data banks of information that permit them to carry out their work in a more informed manner. In hospitals, nurses are being relieved of the chore of acting as a clearing house for information; DRG processors make use of data-base technology to assign diagnosis, and pharmacists, radiologists, and lab personnel gain immediate access to patient information, consult data base sources for appropriate dosages or protocols, and gain assistance through automated recording of procedures and charges. In the city, engineers make use of computer-aided design, tax collectors track down delinquent payers using microcomputers and inspectors record information on handheld computers for subsequent downloading into the main computer. In universities and colleges, librarians are assisted in acquisitions, cataloging, and circulation; scholars consult bibliographies and other data bases, carry out statistical analyses, and utilize microcomputers for writing and communicating with colleagues; development personnel analyze alumni donation patterns; and student information personnel draw upon computerized records for transfers, certification of credits, and preparation of reports.

Middle and upper managerial levels appear to be relatively unaffected as yet, although where microcomputers are utilized for budgeting and portfolio management, they have proved highly useful. Modern systems offer great promise for improved management because old practices based on sketchy information and rule-of-thumb standards can be replaced by modern planning and control techniques in which managers at all levels draw upon far more complete and up-to-date information.

Assessing the Evidence Regarding Employment Effects

The interview evidence regarding employment effects must be assessed with care because in general the organizations studied are in the early stages of putting new-era systems in place. There was little evidence of worker displacement, but the process of bringing in the systems had given rise to a considerable amount of extra work. Moreover, organizations had been able to utilize their existing work force through training, with little need to recruit new personnel, except for a limited number of computer systems specialists and technicians. Yet, the point of utilizing these systems is to permit the organization to function more effectively and to do so at lower cost. The long-term objective, as older workers retire or shift to other employment, is to operate with leaner staffs performing more effectively.

The foregoing does not touch on the impact of the new technology on a considerable number of workers, such as maintenance, kitchen, laundry, and transportation personnel, whose daily work is not directly affected by computers. Thus far such employment does not appear to have been changed, but indirect effects are to be expected. To the extent that management will be enabled to control and schedule operations more closely in coming years, opportunities will arise to reduce employment through reduced staffing and/or greater utilization of part-time personnel. How great such changes will be is impossible to estimate.

Implications for recruitment of lower-level personnel. The implications for future recruitment of lower-level personnel can be summarized briefly. First, there is no indication from the entire body of experience examined herein that any additional lower-level jobs appropriate for the unskilled and poorly educated are being opened up by the new technology. To the contrary, some of the interviewed administrators expected that recruitment standards for lower-level clerical personnel would be somewhat more exacting, with emphasis placed on ability to master computer skills quickly and cope more readily with a broader range of on- the-job problems. Others insisted that current standards were adequate, but these organizations were already drawing almost entirely from applicants with high school training or better.

Second, the occupational composition of nonprofit organizations is changing in ways that are likely to affect adversely the opening up of lower-level jobs. Either because of computerization or for other reasons involving shifting functional emphasis within organizations (e.g., greater emphasis on public relations, more complex relations with government, greater need for computer specialists), the occupational shares accounted for by managers, professionals, and technicians are increasing, and shares accounted for by clerical personnel are decreasing. Here again, there is evidence of a declining demand for workers with marginal educational qualifications.

Opportunities for upward mobility. Opportunities for young workers with high school credentials or less to move upward during their years of employment in nonprofit organizations are not increasing and may well be declining. Large city governments, such as New York City's, have traditionally provided well-established internal labor market opportunities for advancement; hospitals, universities, and colleges have not. With the advent of the new systems and the increased emphasis on technical, professional, and managerial work, there will be a greater emphasis in all these institutions on recruitment from colleges and specialized training institutions and less interest in hiring directly from secondary schools. Applicants without high school diplomas increasingly will find themselves excluded from jobs in these institutions.

The implications for labor market policy are clear. They call for a threefold policy: first, aggressive new efforts to improve secondary school education to raise the level of literacy and numeracy skills and to provide every student with a basic hands-on acquaintance with microcomputers and a general understanding of computer systems; second, a redoubled campaign to reduce the number of high school dropouts; and third, a new set of institutional arrangements to provide opportunities to acquire additional training at any stage of the workers' career.

Implications for minority employment. Hospitals, institutions of higher education, and government at all levels have traditionally been more liberal in their policies of hiring minorities than have private sector organizations, although job openings for these workers have been predominantly in the lower-level occupational categories. Accordingly, the implications of the new trends in work and job opportunity in nonprofit organizations are particularly unfavorable for minority workers.

This, indeed, is a major finding of the study and underscores the importance of the general conclusion that the principal policy changes required by computerization must involve major restructuring of our educational and training institutions. Minorities, with their typically poorer educational background, will find increasing difficulty in gaining access to promising careers in nonprofit organizations unless their educational qualifications and their access to training for upgrading and advancement are significantly improved.

Notes

1. William J. Baumol, "Macroeconomies of Unbalanced Growth: The Anatomy of Urban Crisis," *American Economic Review* 57, 3 (June 1967). Reprinted in Stephen L. Mehay and Geoffrey E. Nann, *Urban Economic Issues* (Glenview, Ill.: Scott, Foresman and Co., 1984), pp. 216–222.

2. Ibid., p. 216.

3. Ibid., p. 217.

4. Ibid., pp. 217–218.

5. This statement does not mean that nonprofit organizations are not labor intensive or that their failure to significantly change these labor-intensive modes of production has not in the past been a primary reason for their rising costs. The analysis that follows questions Baumol's assumption that this condition is inherent in the production of nonprofit services.

6. The remarkable postwar advances in medical technology do not contradict this generalization because they have been directed principally toward providing new methods of diagnosis and treatment rather than increasing labor productivity.

7. John W. Wilson, "Computers: When Will the Slump End?" *Business Week,* April 21, 1986, p. 58.

8. Ibid.

9. Nell P. Eurich, *Corporate Classrooms* (Princeton, N.J.: The Carnegie Foundation of the Advancement for Teaching, 1985).

10. Ibid., p. xi.

11. Ibid.

Appendix A: Selected Examples of Computer Applications from *The Mayor's Management Report, 1984**

Multiagency systems (NYC Productivity Program Section 13–16)

Handheld Microcomputers: Field staff collect information in the handheld computer, which can then be transmitted to central computer system. To be used in various agencies.

Personnel Record System: Automates many steps involved in hiring, transferring, and promoting staff.

Payroll Maintenance System: Replaces the city's manual timekeeping and payroll systems.

Complaint Systems: Used by departments of Environmental Planning, Housing Preservation and Development, and General Services to identify and eliminate duplicate complaints and to generate and track work orders.

CITYNET: A citywide data communications network.

Geosupport System: Assists the field operations of city agencies by processing information on the basis of street address and exact block location.

Fleet Administration and Maintenance Information System: Tracks vehicle, records maintenance history, and updates agencies' vehicle and parts inventory.

Department of Environmental Protection

Emission Source Laboratory (165): Computerizes system for inspecting, licensing, and tracking violations.

---

*Numbers in parentheses indicate page references, *The Mayor's Management Report*, September 17, 1984.

Finance Department

Tax Collection–Computer Matching (528)
Tax Collection–Licenses and Vault Charges (530)
Appraisal System (531)
Procurement System (532)

Fire Department

Computer-Assisted Dispatch System (79)
Critical Information Dispatch System (80)
Information Management System (83)

Department of Health

Health Inspector Productivity and Effectiveness Tracking System (351)
Vital Records Systems (356): Makes birth records immediately available.
Management Systems (356): A variety of systems including hospital
    systems, restaurant control, poison control, and word processing-
    electronic mail systems.

New York City Housing Authority

Inventory Control (NYC productivity program 8)

Human Resources Administration

Public Assistance (456): Electronic Payment File Transfer System to
    elminate check fraud and other check problems.

Law Department

Management Information System (511)
Litigation Support System (512)

Police Department

Computer-Assisted Robbery System (9)

Department of Sanitation

Manpower Forecasting (103)
Manpower Information System (106)

Department of Transportation

Traffic Signal System (143)
Match and Flag System (144): Matches vehicle owners with state's
    computer records to enforce summons.

Appendix B: Two Case Studies of Computerization in Hospitals

New Hanover Memorial Hospital, Wilmington, N.C.

New Hanover Memorial Hospital, a 526-bed general nonprofit community hospital serving as a regional referral center, is of special interest because for the most part it is using only conventional computer technology. Yet, following more than two years of analysis and planning, it is on the brink of introducing major new applications. The present practices of New Hanover Memorial are representative of a large number of institutions; the planned systems reflect the priorities that appear to be developing in many hospitals.

The Present System

The present computerized systems at New Hanover Memorial consist of admissions (ADT), accounting, general ledger, payroll, and billing. The ADT system, which is freestanding, is utilized for both regular and emergency room admissions. It creates patient records and performs a few simple functions (e.g., creates charge cards for use in patient orders, advises pharmacy and housekeeping of admissions, generates simple reports). Payroll and accounting are conventional batch systems with keyboard entry. The billing system also is fed by data entry at terminals in the data center from manually prepared medical reports submitted by ancillary departments. Specialized clerks at terminals answer questions from payers regarding billing. In addition, the hospital has an arrangement with Blue Cross–Blue Shield for direct tape-to-tape transmission of billings.

Other administrative systems, such as inventory control and accounts payable, are paper systems. Communication of doctors' orders for medication and procedures, reports of procedures completed, and prescriptions executed make use of essentially old-time, uncomputerized techniques.[1]

Given the relatively low level of computerization, it is interesting that DRG reporting is assisted by microcomputers utilizing modern software. When patients are discharged, patient files are sent to the Medical Records Department for processing and abstracting. There, a clerk responds to programmed questions on the basis of information in the record, and the computer selects the proper international classification of diseases code and DRG classification.

Personal computers also were utilized in several other departments, including the controllers office for budget and other spread sheet analysis, the industrial manager's office for a variety of projections and special reports, and the nursing department for scheduling of nursing loads in the several stations.

Attempts to control costs under the new prospective payment arrangements have been under way for some time but thus far have focused on lengths of stay. All admissions are screened by a nurse to determine which patients will be treated under Medicare. The expected length of stay is determined from a record of typical nationwide experience for the primary diagnosis, and a follow-up file is created. A longer than the expected stay must be explained by the doctor.

In response to questions regarding the costs of procedures and medications used for DRG reporting, the author was advised that they were supplied by ancillary departments and were not precisely measured by industrial engineers.

The New System

In the fall of 1985, New Hanover Hospital began installation of an HIS data base system with new functions for admissions and order entry retrieval capability. When the system is completed terminals will be available in nurses stations and in all departments. Doctors will give orders to nurses stations for entry. After entry, they will be printed out in the ancillary departments.[2] Departments will be computer assisted. For example, in the laboratory a report will be generated when blood serum is processed, and in the pharmacy the computer will check for possible interactions between drugs prescribed, print labels, and keep track of inventory. All departments will be able to access patient records, and all reports of ancillary departments will be available immediately to nurses and doctors at terminals. Doctors also will be able to access such information through PCs connected by telephone lines to their homes and offices.

Although these are the immediate changes, other changes are in the wings. A computerized inventory control system is planned once the HIS system is in place, and a number of sophisticated applications, such as computerization of operating room reporting and development of standard costs are under consideration.

Anticipated employment changes include the elimination of twenty-five to thirty clerical jobs out of a total employment of more than 1,700 persons. It is also expected that nursing duties will change somewhat. On one hand, the order entry system will make information on results of procedures and tests available to doctors on terminals so that nurses will no longer have to answer queries. On the other hand, nurses will be expected to enter the physician orders on terminals initially, thereby adding to their duties.[3]

The system is expected to cost $2 million for hardware and software during the next five years. Direct savings are expected to come principally from the reduction in clerical personnel, but the system is considered essential for coping with the problems of prospective payment by establishing physician profiles of treatment and working with attending physicians to reduce costs. In addition, management sees as a major general objective an improvement in the level of medical care through increasing efficiency.

Hospital Corporation of America (HCA)

HCA is the leading operator of proprietary hospitals; it owns or leases 184 acute care centers (30,402 beds) and thirty-six psychiatric hospitals (4,449 beds) in the United States and twenty-five international facilities (2,220 beds). In addition, HCA manages 188 facilities in the United States and abroad. Examination of HCA's recent and current experience with computerization and its future plans provides insight into the way in which large multiunit private sector organizations are currently using technology. This examination also suggests the types of new applications that are being given first priority for adoption in the near future. At the same time, it provides evidence of the strategy of at least one major organization in coping with the rapidly changing environment.

The HCA Computer Systems

During the 1970s, computerization of HCA hospitals featured a time-sharing arrangement in which finance, payroll, and basic patient accounting information for all hospitals were processed daily in batch mode at a central facility (General Electric in Rockville, Md.). Computerization varied to some extent among hospitals but for the most part was limited to business functions and essential patient ADT information. As one executive noted, "The big strength in consolidation was that all the numbers were rolled up and used by different levels of management."

During the early 1980s, HCA mapped out the basic architecture of an expanded and largely new approach to computerization. This approach calls for a distributed system at the hospital level that consists of independent functional systems (business support, patient logistics, material management, nursing administration, laboratory, pharmacy, radiology, hospital communication, and physician support), each equipped with a minicomputer and linked to other systems within the hospital through a local area network (LAN). The distributed system will be linked to the central HCA shared applications system through a nationwide area network. The HCA shared applications system when complete will provide for quantitative management (operating information control, budgeting), general accounting (general ledger, accounts payable, payroll control), shared applications (accounts receivable, inpatient billing), and medical reporting (DRG utilization and financial reporting, medical staff performances, DRG component structure, patient origin). When the overall system is completed, individual hospitals will be able to download financial and clerical information from the central data bases in order to improve operational efficiency and patient care.[4]

The program is at once amibitious and pragmatic. On one hand, HCA visualizes as its ultimate target a highly complex and sophisticated computerization effort that will support all aspects of hospital operations and provide maximum assistance to management at all levels. On the other, HCA is willing to proceed with caution, one step at a time, to assure that systems meet user needs and operate efficiently.[5]

The strategy behind the system. Discussions with management along with a visit to Westside Hospital in Nashville, the 250-bed facility in which the largest number of new systems are deployed, made it clear that the development of computer systems in HCA was guided not only by an avowed philosophy of improving management and operational efficiency at all levels and of taking full advantage of economies of scale but by a strategy for coping with the new health care environment. This strategy focuses on providing computer support to increase productivity of the basic functions of the hospital; improving utilization review procedures and speeding up the process of diagnosis and the ordering of medication and procedures; and moving expeditiously into the development of total health care systems.

It is clear that first priority has been given to meeting the needs of its many small- and medium-sized hospitals by developing computer support for the key ancillary departments. At Westside, business office support, pharmacy, and materials management systems (each with its dedicated minicomputer) are fully or substantially operational, and inpatient subsystems for medical records, radiology, nursing administration, and personnel are also in use.[6] It is interesting that HCA has moved to make each system or subsystem operational without waiting for the completion of the LAN network (which in late summer 1985 was still in the pilot stage of development). Member hospitals are urged to move toward installation at their own pace and according to their own needs. Many elements of the total system, for example, the physician's support system, remain under development.

The priority given to computerization at the departmental level is an indication that HCA is emphasizing across-the-board cost reduction as its major strategy in coping with increasing competition and the pressures of prospective pricing. But it also may be an indication that a large number of HCA-member hospitals, most of which are relatively small, simply do not have computerized systems (or at least sophisticated systems) in their ancillary departments. If the latter is true, it is very probable that the state of computerization in HCA hospitals also represents the level of sophistication of a large number of smaller hospitals that are not a part of the HCA organization.

Notwithstanding this emphasis on building basic systems, management emphasized repeatedly that careful utilization review at both the hospital and corporate levels lay at the heart of operating successfully in a prospective payment environment. Although specific procedural arrangements were not discussed, an essential element of the strategy was to classify properly each illness. HCA holds that the DRG classification used by Medicare is inappropriate for utilization review because it contains insufficient information regarding complications as well as other pertinent data. As one executive noted, "You can't sit down with a doctor and talk about a case in terms of DRG. He's going to insist that you recognize more specific conditions."

For this reason HCA has devised a more detailed DRG classification known as patient diagnostic categories (PDC) and has developed software for use with a PC to facilitate PDC classification of each patient's treatment. Hardware and software are available to each member hospital. At the corporate level the system accumulates information on experience and costs that provides a basis for monitoring hospital performance as well as a set of standards against which the hospital's utilization review procedures can take place.[7]

Along with utilization review, a major HCA effort is to reduce the length of patient stays by expediting the flow of clinical information to and from the attending physician. HCA maintains that a day of hospitalization is typically lost in preliminary testing and the time it takes to deliver this information to the physician so that he or she can design an effective treatment. Accordingly, HCA is developing (in addition to the hospital order-entry system) a support system for the doctor's office that will permit him or her to access information on the patient's admission, to order tests, receive reports, and monitor patients throughout their hospital stay. In order to induce physicians to install necessary facilities, HCA plans to offer an entire system at a bargain-basement price (IBM PC-AT and software) that not only will tie in with the hospital but also will support management of physicians' offices and provide them with access to clinical information data banks and other information resources.

Finally, HCA sees the changing environment as one in which two major sets of change are occurring at once, each related to the other. The first is the movement toward prospective payment arrangements as the prevailing mode—not only for Medicare payment but for third-party contractual arrangements of all kinds and for individual payment plans as well. The second is the growth of the total health care system to embrace hospitals, doctors' offices, outpatient clinics, intermediate care facilities, nursing homes, and home care. HCA sees its competitive strength in this new environment as a function of size, managerial strength, and the development of its information system. Size and managerial strength permit HCA to assume the insurance risks implicit in prospective payment arrangements. Under prospective payment, individual hospitals, no matter how well run, are vulnerable to the effects of an unfavorable case mix, whereas large systems can offset unavoidable high cost experiences in some facilities with favorable experiences elsewhere in the system. Size also enables HCA to operate total health care systems, which in turn make possible lower treatment costs because patients can be assigned to the appropriate treatment arrangement (e.g., shifting the patient from hospitals to lower-cost intermediate facilities or home care treatment). Finally, the development of large information systems permits a more effective control of costs and collection of revenues as well as the development of a body of clinical information that improves the quality of health care. At present, HCA is beginning to move into all of these new areas—health maintenance organizations, preferred provider organizations, and the development of total health care systems.

Employment Effects Within HCA

The HCA experience demonstrates how difficult it is to trace the impact of computerization on employment. At the outset, the corporation intended to save "one full-time employee with each new departmental system installed in addition to gaining new information." In practice, however, it has been difficult to determine whether the objective had been achieved. There have been reductions in employment and changing patterns of employment due to a number of changes, including the declining demand for hospital care and the increased efficiency arising out of new managerial initiatives. Moreover, there have been some increases in demand for labor, at least in the short run. During the changeover period, there is a need for additional labor hours to enter information from paper records into computer memory, to maintain old and new systems side by side, and to engage in training activities.

Nevertheless, it is clear that the new systems have reduced the need for certain kinds of work. The pharmacy system, for example, automates the typing of labels for medication and IV prescriptions; reduces labor involved in preparing the carts of medication by generating fill lists; provides for automatic changing and automatic pricing updates; screens automatically for allergies, drug interactions, and duplicate drug orders; and generates medication schedules for nursing and reduces the task of inventory management. A similar list of labor-saving innovations could be provided for each department affected, especially in laboratory, ADT functions, materials management, nursing management, and payroll. The installation of the automatic time clock, which is on line to the national networked accounting system, is perhaps the most dramatic example because the time clock reduces in every department the administrative task of reporting time and pay rates and adjusting for shift differentials and overtime.

Moreover, there remains a significant potential for further reduction of work as additional parts of the total system—especially the order entry system, which is still in the pilot stage of development—are put in place. At Westside Hospital it was clear that there was a considerable amount of clerical work that remained to be eliminated. For example, all orders for medication and procedures and all departmental reports (except pharmacy reports which are automatically transmitted via telephone line) continue to be prepared and transmitted in the conventional manner. There is also a certain amount of repetitive data entry (e.g., DRG reports to Medicare are prepared separately rather than as a byproduct of the medical records data entry and abstracting process). Demands for results of laboratory tests, x-rays, and the like continue to be funneled into the nursing station in the traditional way and with the traditional interruption of nurses' other duties.

The question was raised with several middle-level managers involved in information system administration as to how much work was being changed and whether or not more was demanded of workers and management. The executives agreed readily that lower-level work was being eliminated and that new work often involved a wider range of responsibility, although it might be simplified by computer assistance.[8]

It was not clear from their experience of HCA, however, that there had as yet been a significant change in the type of person being hired or that persons whose duties were eliminated by computerization could not be utilized elsewhere within the organization.

A final issue is the effect of computerization on organization and through organization on employment. It is intriguing that HCA is at present implementing its planned system with little apparent organizational change at least at the hospital level. Its strategy is to move first toward meeting the needs of its member hospitals (mostly small and almost entirely nonteaching) for computer support in existing departments and toward putting in place the essential managerial arrangements and computer equipment to enable hospitals to begin operating in a more competitive environment.

Notes

1. One approach considered unique by New Hanover Memorial is to conserve nurses' time by xeroxing the doctors written orders. The original is then passed by pneumatic tube to a clerical department where clerks manually execute requisitions for medication and procedures.

2. Direct entry by doctors would be possible, but hospital administrators do not believe that doctors will enter orders themselves. Note: The State of North Carolina permits electronic orders and signature for purposes of the medical record.

3. Under present arrangements nurses simply xerox the doctors' orders and send a copy by pneumatic tube to a clerical station for forwarding.

4. This sketch of the major elements of HCA's planned systems is as presented in HCA Network Exchange, *HCA Computer Systems*, July 1985.

5. At the corporate level the developmental process involves extensive evaluation of each user's need and available external systems. Company policy does not eschew use of other vendor systems but at the same time calls for internal development of systems or modification of outside systems in order to fully meet user requirements and to assure independence of vendors in final operation. Systems are fully tested in pilot installations and then at "first cycle" deployment sites before being offered to user hospitals at large. Individual hospitals are encouraged to proceed in adoption at their own pace and are given assistance by experienced teams at every stage of installation and activation.

6. Westside shares a freestanding laboratory with several other hospitals.

7. It is interesting that although HCA is moving aggressively to reduce costs through departmental computer systems and through installation of utilization review, it has not yet elected to mount an effort to determine the standard costs of laboratory procedures, radiology, and so on. Management's reply to queries regarding cost determination was that it would be very expensive and "probably not worth it" at this stage of its effort.

8. One executive pointed out that in pharmacy there has been a sharp reduction in low-level duties but an increased demand for the services of the professional pharmacist who executes the order system and must deal with information the system generates regarding drug incompatibility and the like. Here the system brings with it a new level of quality of performance and places new demands on personnel.

Appendix C: A Case Study of Computerization in Universities and Colleges

Stevens Institute of Technology

Stevens Institute of Technology in Hoboken, N.J., is an old and highly reputable institution (1,600 undergraduate and 1,400 graduate students) that offers degree programs in mathematics, physics, chemistry, management, computer science, and various fields of engineering.

Academic Computing

After a review of the institute's program in the late 1970s, Stevens officials concluded that it was important that computers play a larger role in its educational program but that there was no room in the curriculum for additional courses. A nationwide study of engineering schools carried out by Stevens in 1979 revealed that most engineering students were required to learn programming in their freshman year but did not apply their skills until the junior or senior year. Moreover, no engineering schools were found to have begun to frame a strategy for the introduction of computer-assisted instruction (CAI) throughout their academic programs.[1] Following this survey Stevens began to develop its own program, one that would "weave a computer thread" into the core of required courses. In 1980, Stevens initiated its Computers in Engineering Education Project.

The program's objective was to train the Stevens student to become computer fluent and to turn to the computer when appropriate. Likewise, the institute intended to equip its students with the ability to identify the capabilities and limitations of computer systems and software, to develop higher level language programs for engineering problems, and to implement professional techniques including numerical methods, modeling simulation, computer graphics, data acquisition, and process control. Twenty-five freshmen courses were scheduled for revision, and changes also were planned for some junior and senior level courses.

The immediate impact of the new program was to increase computer use by 30 percent and to seriously overload existing computer facilities. The administration then decided to require that students own personal computers, which were to be used in at least one course each semester through the junior year. An ATARI personal computer system was selected for purchase at a cost of $800. The program was implemented first in the science, computer science, and management departments.

The program was so successful that it was expanded immediately to engineering, extended to the senior year, and students were required to purchase a more powerful microcomputer. Each member of the freshman class of 1983–1984 purchased, at a cost of $1,800 (heavily discounted), a DEC PC 325, thereby making Stevens the first institution in the United States to require that new students own computers. At the same time, the school mounted a major effort to prepare for the new program. Computer warehousing and maintenance facilities were established, and dormitory rooms were renovated to accommodate the new equipment. Faculty members working with graduate students and undergraduate programmers developed CAI programs to be used in freshman calculus, chemistry, physics, and introductory engineering-graphics courses; programs included homework exercises, tutorials, and simulations. The computers were used in classrooms as well as in dormitories.Lectures and labs were enhanced by interactive drills and tutorials, and computers were introduced into several humanities courses (humanities students were required to use word processing software to write essays). At present, the campus is not networked, but the institution is moving toward implementation of a highly advanced telecommunications system.

The library. Stevens is an illustration of the way in which a medium-sized library with a limited budget brings about automation of its operations and services. By subscribing to RLIN as a nonmember search-only user, the library is able to use a major bibliographic data base for assistance in acquisitions, but it does not have automated acquisition procedures. The library does, however, use a personal computer to generate purchase orders and to track orders and deliveries. Cataloging is largely automated, and the card catalog is being converted to machine readable format. On-line catalog services are not available because a suitable system has not yet been located. The Stevens librarian complained that there are adequate systems for small libraries and for very large libraries, but as yet no system has been found that meets Stevens' requirements.

The Stevens library installed on-line retrieval systems more than a decade ago that offered a full range of DIALOG data bases for literature search. In handling interlibrary loan requirements the library utilizes the RLIN data base to locate lenders, but otherwise arrangements for securing loans are not computer assisted.

Administrative Computing

Although administrative computing at Stevens has not received the emphasis given to the academic program, there have been important improvements in several of the Stevens systems in recent years, and one of the big eight accounting firms has been contracted to plan and put in place a modern integrated administrative system. The three major systems that are significantly modernized are student information, payroll and personnel, and financial accounting. The student records system, which has been in use for several years, records grades by mark-sense readers, electronically processes student grade averages, course requirements, and so on, and produces printouts of academic records for review. Payroll and personnel systems are integrated using a separate minicomputer-based system. They are not, however, integrated with the main computer, and only limited on-line access is available. The present financial and accounting system, which was introduced in 1984, has on-line capability that is utilized for developmental analysis, but it is largely batch fed. In addition, there is a financial aid system with on-line inquiry capability and an alumni records system. Finally, Stevens makes considerable use of word processing, with "word processors on almost every desk."

Employment Effects

Employment and enrollment data provide a clear picture of trends in recent years and are consistent with information provided in the interviews (Table C.1).

Student enrollment at Stevens grew sharply (26 percent) during the period 1977–1985, especially in graduate programs (37 percent), where an aggressive program of recruitment was carried out. Total employment showed much smaller gains (12 percent), however, with some very different trends noted among the several classifications. The professional nonfaculty and technical/professional groups increased by 30 percent or more, principally because of the addition of computing technical staff and the need for additional professionals in accounting and development (including recruitment for the new management program). The service maintenance staff also was enlarged to accommodate the new program for student-owned computers. The executive/managerial group was reduced, however, in part through reorganization. The skilled crafts

TABLE C.1

Staff	1977	1985	Percentage Change
Faculty	129	154	19.4
Executive/administrative/managerial	68	64	−10.6
Professional nonfaculty	38	51	34.2
Technical/paraprofessional	23	30	30.4
Secretarial/clerical	120	130	8.3
Skilled crafts	36	28	−22.2
Service/maintenance	109	127	16.5
Total	523	584	11.7
Student Enrollment			
Undergraduate	1,292	1,512	17.2
Graduate	973	1,335*	37.2
Total	2,265	2,847	25.7

*Additional 600 students in off-campus programs.

Source: Data provided by Stevens Institute management.

personnel were also reduced, but for reasons not made clear in the interviews.

What is perhaps most interesting from the viewpoint of this study is that secretarial/clerical employment grew by only 8 percent. This is fully consistent with the discussion with executives at Stevens. The widespread use of word processing plus greater utilization of computerized systems simply made it possible to process a much heavier load of administrative work with only a slightly larger staff.

There was considerable discussion in the interviews of how and how much the nature of work had changed. In general, it was maintained that computerization simplified work. An example, offered by the executive vice president of academic affairs, was the elimination of the need for highly skilled typists. In years past, he pointed out, a typist with the skills to type important or intricate documents was difficult to replace. The loss of one was cause for alarm. Now, however, the specialty no longer exists. With word processing any of a number of persons in any office can be called on for such work. When hired, new personnel are advised that anyone who performs tasks requiring typing will be expected to use word processors. If new employees are not familiar with the equipment, they are trained on the job. In general, on-the-job training of all clerical administrative personnel was said to be carried out systematically but informally and was considered highly effective.

In response to the question, "Are you looking for anything different (from earlier years) when you hire lower level personnel?" the answer was in the negative. Again, it was noted that technology simplified tasks, and no greater skill was required. For clerical work no more than a high school diploma was required, and even that was not strictly necessary.

But at the same time, the director of personnel observed that applicants for jobs had changed in recent years. A greater number came from technical schools or had word processing skills developed in secretarial schools. There were "more and more with credentials." In hiring, "we do look at these skills although they are not necessary."

Stevens appears to draw upon an abundant labor market. There are many who prefer to work close to home in Hoboken and in the attractive surroundings of the Stevens campus rather than commute to Manhattan. The Stevens pay scale is relatively low, but, apparently, there are compensations.

Opportunities for advancement appear to be limited. Among clerical and secretarial personnel, there was an aggressive effort through on-the-job training to move lower-level employees to the middle level where virtually all the turnover was taking place. Upper-level workers in this occupational class had for the most part been employed by the college for many years.

There was also very little movement into the professional or managerial ranks. Here new personnel were brought in from the outside. Outside recruitment included an assistant controller (from the Princeton University staff), a budget manager (from industry), an internal auditor (recently retired from an accounting firm), a manager of user services (a recent MBA from Syracuse University), and several experienced Stevens graduate students (who were receiving tuition remission) who were hired for technical posts.

Notes

1. The account of Stevens Institute's academic program is based on a presentation by Dr. Edward Freedman, Academic Vice President, Stevens Institute, at Columbia University on January 2, 1985 and a subsequent interview, as well as an article by Carol Thorsten-Stein, "Making the Grade," *Digital Review*, September 1984.

Index

Date Due

BRODART, INC.   Cat. No. 23 233   Printed in U.S.A.